THE BYZANTINE
CHURCHES
OF ISTANBUL
A Photographic Survey

THE BYZANTINE CHURCHES OF ISTANBUL
A Photographic Survey

Thomas F. Mathews

The Pennsylvania State University Press
University Park and London

Plans and map prepared by Glenn Ruby and Robert Texter.

Library of Congress Cataloging in Publication Data

Mathews, Thomas F.
    The Byzantine churches of Istanbul.

    Includes index.
    1. Istanbul—Churches—Pictorial works. 2. Architecture, Byzantine—Istanbul. 3. Church architecture—Istanbul. I. Title.
NA5870.A1M37   726'.5'094961   75-27173
ISBN 0-271-01210-2

Copyright © 1976 The Pennsylvania State University
All rights reserved

Designed by Glenn Ruby

Printed in the United States of America
by Meriden Gravure

Frontispiece: Christos tēs Chōras

To Zena, my wife

Contents

Acknowledgments		ix
List of Principal Abbreviations		xi
Introduction		xiii

The Churches

1	Hag. Andreas en tē Krisei	3
2	Atik Mustafa Paşa Camii	15
3	Aykapı	23
4	Balaban Ağa Mescidi	25
5	Beyazit Churches A, B, and C	28
6	Beyazit Church D	34
7	Bogdan Sarayı	36
8	Christos tēs Chōras	40
9	Christos ho Pantepoptēs	59
10	Christos ho Pantokratōr	71
11	Hag. Eirēnē	102
12	Hag. Euphēmia en tō Hippodromō	123
13	Gül Camii	128
14	Hag. Iōannēs Prodromos en tō Hebdomō	140
15	Hag. Iōannēs Prodromos en tois Stoudiou	143
16	Hag. Iōannēs Prodromos en tō Troullō	159
17	Isa Kapısı Mescidi	168
18	Kalenderhane Camii	171
19	Kasim Ağa Mescidi	186
20	Kefeli Mescidi	190
21	Manastır Mescidi	195
22	Mangana Churches	200

23	Hag. Mēnas	206
24	Myrelaion	209
25	Odalar Camii	220
26	Hag. Polyeuktos	225
27	Sancaktar Hayreddin Mescidi	231
28	Sekbanbaşı Mescidi	237
29	Hag. Sergios kai Bakchos en tois Hormisdou	242
30	Sinan Paşa Mescidi	260
31	Hagia Sophia	262
32	Şeyh Murat Mescidi	313
33	Şeyh Süleyman Mescidi	315
34	Theotokos tōn Chalkoprateiōn	319
35	Theotokos tou Libos	322
36	Theotokos hē Pammakaristos	346
37	Theotokos hē Panagiotissa	366
38	Toklu Dede Mescidi	376
39	Topkapı Sarayı Basilica	383
40	Vefa Kilise Camii	386
Index		403

Acknowledgments

Compiling this survey has afforded many pleasures, not the least of which derived from the generosity I encountered among many colleagues who assisted me one way or another in the work. It is a pleasure to recall my association with them and my debts to them.

In the first place I must thank the authorities in charge of the Byzantine monuments of Istanbul whose permissions made my photographing possible. Access to the monuments under their care was liberally accorded me by Ihsan Erzi, the director of the Vakiflar, Ministry of Mosques; by Necati Dolunay, director of the Istanbul Archaeological Museum; by Feridun Dirimtekin and his successor Hâdi Altai, directors of the Hagia Sophia Museum; and by Very Reverend Kallinikos of the Orthodox Patriarchate in Istanbul.

Byzantine scholars and archaeologists have also been extremely helpful in many different ways. I am especially appreciative of the assistance of Nezih Fıratlı of the Istanbul Archaeological Museum; Richard Hamann-MacLean, the University of Mainz; R. Martin Harrison, the University of Newcastle-upon-Tyne; Ernest Hawkins, Dumbarton Oaks Center for Byzantine Studies; Ernst Kitzinger, Harvard University; Doğan Kuban, the Istanbul Technical University; Cyril Mango, Exeter College, Oxford; Arif Mufit Mansel, the University of Istanbul; Donald Nicol, King's College, University of London; Urs Peschlow, the German Archaeological Institute in Istanbul; and Robert Van Nice, Dumbarton Oaks Center for Byzantine Studies. I am particularly indebted, however, to Richard Krautheimer of the Institute of Fine Arts, New York University, and C.L. Striker of the University of Pennsylvania. I relied on their encouragement and advice season after season and I hope my work reflects the high standards they set for their own.

I would like to express my thanks as well for the library and archive facilities made available to me. I would like to thank Bekir Sükrü Eğeli, secretary of the Eski Eserleri Koruma Encümeni; D.E. Dean, librarian of the Royal Institute of British Architects; W.M. Freitag, librarian of the Fogg Art Museum of Harvard University; M. Eliot, librarian of Burrows Library of Byzantine and Modern Greek, King's College, University of London; Judith O'Neill, photoarchivist of Dumbarton Oaks Center for Byzantine Studies; Josephine Powell, photographer, Rome; and M. von Stockhausen of Bildarchiv Foto Marburg.

For bibliographical and editorial assistance I had the capable help of Ellen C. Schwartz, Zoran Tosič, and Grace Van Hulsteyn.

For financial aid in the project I am grateful to the Samuel H. Kress Foundation for post-doctoral grants in 1969 and 1970, and to the City University of New York for a new-faculty grant in 1971.

Finally I must acknowledge the occasional help of a very knowledgeable guide, Bilgin Turnali, the patience of countless imams, muezzins, and custodians, and the hospitality of all those in Istanbul who welcomed me on their balconies, chimneys, and rooftops in search of better views of Istanbul's churches.

List of Principal Abbreviations

AA	*Archäologischer Anzeiger*
AB	*The Art Bulletin*
AJA	*American Journal of Archaeology*
BZ	*Byzantinische Zeitschrift*
CA	*Cahiers archéologiques*
DOP	*Dumbarton Oaks Papers*
Ebersolt and Thiers, *Les églises*	J. Ebersolt and A. Thiers, *Les églises de Constantinople* (Paris, 1913)
EO	*Echos d'Orient*
Eyice, *Son Devir Bizans Mimarisi*	Semavi Eyice, *Son Devir Bizans Mimarisi: Istanbul'da Palaiologoslar Devri Anıtları* (Istanbul, 1969).
IM	*Istanbuler Mitteilungen*
Janin, *Géographie*	R. Janin, *La géographie ecclésiastique de l'empire byzantin: Constantinople, Les églises et les monastères* (Paris, 1969)
Krautheimer, *Early Christian and Byzantine Architecture*	Richard Krautheimer, *Early Christian and Byzantine Architecture* (Baltimore, 1965)
Mathews, *The Early Churches of Constantinople*	T.F. Mathews, *The Early Churches of Constantinople: Architecture and Liturgy* (University Park, Pa. 1971)
Paspates, *Byzantinai meletai*	A.G. Paspates, *Byzantinai meletai topographikai kai historikai* (Constantinople, 1877)
REB	*Revue des études byzantins*
Schneider, *Byzanz*	A.M. Schneider, *Byzanz: Vorarbeiten zur Topographie und Archäologie der Stadt*, Istanbuler Forschungen, 8 (Berlin, 1936)
Van Millingen, *Byzantine Churches*	A. Van Millingen, *Byzantine Churches in Constantinople, Their History and Architecture* (London, 1912)

Introduction

The purpose of this work is to present to the scholar or student of Byzantine architecture a reasonably complete photographic documentation of the churches of ancient Constantinople. This is not a history of Byzantine architecture in the capital, as desirable as that might be, but a visual record of the monuments on which such a history might be based; for the history of architecture is not a speculative discipline but a factual, descriptive science, the first task of which is to trace the succession of physical monuments and describe their evolution. Only on this kind of brick-and-mortar basis can the historian safely proceed to the subsequent work of interpreting the monuments in their broader cultural setting. This book, then, is intended as a research tool, a reference work that will facilitate the serious study of Istanbul's ancient monuments by making available in a single volume a handy archive of photographic information.

Most of the photographs in the present volume have not been published before, and most of them were taken expressly for this survey in the hope of compiling coverage that would be reasonably uniform and complete. The study of Byzantine architecture in Istanbul has varied enormously from monument to monument, from the cursory observations of interested travelers to the systematic research of professional archaeologists. The photographic coverage has been correspondingly uneven. While Justinian's cathedral of Hagia Sophia is one of the most photographed buildings in the world, other monuments have been so neglected that one would have trouble locating even two or three published photographs that are reliable and informative. The most thorough coverage attempted in a single volume is that of Alexander Van Millingen, who in 1912 described twenty-two churches in some hundred and fifty photographs.[1] Indispensable as his work is, its photographic coverage was far from complete in its own day and a much wider range of material has come to light since then. The archaeological exploration of Istanbul has almost doubled the number of known Byzantine monuments (the present survey counts forty entries, many of them multiple entries), and cleaning and restoration has revealed much of the original architecture that was hidden from view in Van Millingen's time. Encumbering additions have been removed from many of the monuments, wall surfaces and sculptural details exposed by the stripping away of layers of plaster, pavements uncovered, stolen columns replaced, and rooflines returned to their original profiles. While some of this evidence has been made available in scattered archaeological reports, much of it has remained unknown. This volume was undertaken to provide a fresh photographic survey that would record the present state of the monuments in a more systematic fashion than has been attempted before.

Older photographic documentation, however, cannot be neglected. The alterations of recent years have not all been to our advantage. Some monuments have deteriorated badly, others have disappeared entirely before the relentless pressures of twentieth century living, and still others have fallen victim to excessive restoration that has irretrievably erased valuable archaeological information. Older photographs, therefore, will always be indispensable to the study of the Istanbul monuments, and whenever such photographs could be obtained that witness more faithfully the original fabric of the churches they have been included in this survey.

It is remarkable how much of this valuable documentation of older photographs has remained unpublished and virtually unconsulted in archives, where, doubtless, many more discoveries remain to be made. Three archives especially deserve mention in this connection. The oldest and most important is the collection of the Eski Eserleri Koruma Encümeni (the Society for the Preservation of Ancient Monuments), housed in the Istanbul Archaeological Museum. Begun in 1910 and enlarged over the years, this archive embraces all the historical monuments of Istanbul, Turkish and Byzantine, and constitutes an inestimable resource for the student of Istanbul, including at present over thirteen hundred monuments. European scholars, unfortunately, have remained virtually unaware of its existence. Similar in scope, although less comprehensive, is the archive of the German Archaeological Institute in Istanbul, begun in 1932. The most extensive photographic collection devoted exclusively to the Byzantine monuments is the archive of the Dumbarton Oaks Center for Byzantine Studies in Washington, D.C. Here the records of excavation and restoration projects of the Byzantine Institute of the United States and of the Dumbarton Oaks Field Committee have been filed since 1940. To this vast store has been added in recent years the invaluable collection of Nicholas V. Artamonoff, who independently photographed many of the churches in the late 1930s. In addition to these three archives, other important original material has been found in the photo archive of the Fogg Art Museum of Harvard University, which includes an extensive collection assembled by Arthur Kingsley Porter in the 1920s, and in the Bildarchiv Foto Marburg, in Germany.

The 655 photographs presented here, then, have been edited from a collection of some 10,000 taken by the author as well as from thousands more examined in archives. The material has been selected primarily with a view to comprehensive coverage, as far as is possible in a single volume. General views, interior and exterior, ought to present each important aspect of the building, while details ought to show significant particulars of structure, masonry, or decoration (exclusive, however, of fresco and mosaic decoration which for the most part have been adequately published elsewhere). Ideally, one ought to be able to follow in such a collection the sequence of spaces in each church from narthex to sanctuary; one should be able to examine the different kinds of vaulting, the handling of surfaces, the cutting of sculptural ornament, or the subtleties of lighting, where these elements have not been drastically altered. On the other hand, comparing monument to monument one could trace the evolution of a motif over the centuries or establish the consistency of stylistic features at a given moment.

The problem of comprehensive coverage, however, is much more complex than this statement of objectives might convey. No collection of photographs, however extensive, can substitute for first-hand inspection of the building, and no set of photographs can claim to represent its definitive portrait. Architecture always proves more subtle and more elusive than one expects. The task of architectural photography is not the recording of masonry, meter by meter, but of architecture, which is something more. More than walls, the photographer must see the volumes, the mass, the proportions of a building; he must have an eye for the abstract play of shapes and lines, their variations and development from part to part of the building; he must notice the modulations of surface, whether flat or folded, cornered or concave; and he must observe the changing role of ornamentation from the severe and geometric to the rich and fanciful, teeming with plants that do not grow on earth and birds that never fly. Most critical of all, the photographer must study the play of light and shadow—on the outside, the conditions of sun and cloud that shift with the hours of the day and the seasons of the year; and on the inside, the calculated light controlled by the architect, whether it flares through narrow slits or floods in through wide arches or filters evenly down from a ring of windows in a drum.

Conceived in these terms, the goal of comprehensive photographic documentation becomes more and more chimerical. Photography's reputation as a factual and objective medium is highly misleading. Every set of photographs represents the interpretation of the photographer who took them, and every set of photographs represents a transformation of the object through the camera's way of seeing. In fact, it is only when the archaeologist has accepted the subjectivity of the camera that he can use the camera to its full advantage. He can then accept a view of the building from above, for example, without apologizing for the fact that the original architect never saw it except from the ground; he can pick out a detail with a telephoto lens that would have been scarcely visible from the ordinary viewer's vantage; or he can set the camera on its back and spread out the vaults above in a dizzying wide angle. Photography cannot reproduce the art of the architect; we can hope, however, that the photographer's art will somehow illuminate the art of the architect.

Certain boundaries have had to be observed in compiling this survey. In the first place the material has been restricted to churches, a term which includes, for present purposes, all structures identifiable as somehow ecclesiastical, whether they be churches and chapels, as most of them are, or baptisteries, hagiasmas, mausolea, skeuophylakia, martyria, or monasteries.[2] This, of course, comprises only one part of the architectural achievement of ancient Constantinople. The surviving civic architecture, however, including the city walls, the aqueducts and cisterns, palace fragments, the hippodrome, and the honorific monuments, leave little to photograph that has not already been extensively surveyed. Moreover the churches form a fairly natural unit by themselves, with their own distinctive problems and their own distinctive design solutions.

Chronologically the survey embraces the churches of Constantinople from Constantine's founding of the capital to the Turkish Conquest of 1453. It should be borne in mind, however, that of the hundreds of known churches only those are included, whether standing or ruined, of which photographic documentation can be compiled. The photographic coverage has been stretched in a few instances to include occasional drawings and engravings of the nineteenth century when their scientific value seemed reliable and their evidence could not be duplicated in photographs. On the other hand, representations in medieval maps and miniatures are usually too schematic to be used as archaeological evidence without extensive interpretation and commentary, and therefore they have been omitted. Inevitably, then, some of the most famous historical monuments of the city will not be found here, such as Justinian's five-domed church of the Holy Apostles that served as imperial mausoleum for centuries, or the Blachernēs basilica of the Mother-of-God that was so important to pilgrims. Their ruins still lie buried and unidentified, and although scattered fragments have turned up that may conjecturally be assigned to such monuments, they do not seem worth including until they can be securely attached to the site to which they belong.

The geographical limits of the survey are perhaps not as self-evident as the chronological. The boundaries of Constantinople might be drawn, with Procopius, to include the suburbs along the Marmara and the Bosporus on both the Asiatic and European coasts. Dealing with ecclesiastical architecture, however, it seemed logical to accept the ecclesiastical boundaries of the city as defined by Raymond Janin, namely, the city itself and its European suburbs that fell under the jurisdiction of the same metropolitan and belonged to the eparchy of Constantinople.[3] Crossing the Bosporus one would enter the diocese of Chalcedon. The Asiatic shore, therefore, and the Princes' Islands are omitted.[4] On the European side, moreover, the survey has not gone beyond the suburb of Hebdomon; to go further would be to make all of Thrace part of the city, which hardly seems logical.

The entry for each church in the survey comprises, in addition to the photographs themselves, a plan of the church, a bibliography, and a brief introduction. These are included to increase the usefulness of the photographs. Architectural photographs are very difficult to use without plans that provide some orientation and sense of direction. That fresh architectural plans ought to be made of many of the monuments will be immediately evident, but this seemed to lie beyond the scope of the present survey, and since the plans here are meant only as keys to the photographs it was hoped that reusing the best published plans would fill the purpose.[5] On each plan numbered arrows indicate the approximate angle of each photograph (consult the key on p. xx). It should be noticed that indications of direction in the captions of the photographs do not always correspond to the compass indication on the plans; instead, for the sake of simplicity the captions follow the common convention of assuming that the apse end of the church points due east.[6] A map of church locations has been included, but since a complete topographical study of the monuments of Istanbul is now in preparation by Wolfgang Müller-Wiener, more exact topographical information seemed unnecessary here.

The bibliography and introduction that accompany each entry are also meant as aids to understanding the photographs. Each bibliography is arranged in chronological order to follow the development of research on the church down to the present; it does not attempt to collect all possible references to the monument, but lists instead only studies that have made a real contribution to the progress of study. The introductory text, on the other hand, is intended more as commentary on the bibliography than as a new contribution to research in its own right. An attempt has been made to give some account of the present condition of the monument, and to present a critical review of the present state of research on that monument. The intent is to help focus attention on the real issues involved in the plates.[7]

The entries have been arranged in alphabetical order, and this too involves evaluation of the present state of research. One of the most persistent problems in the archaeology of Istanbul has always been the correct Byzantine identification of the surviving monuments: one cannot even name a monument without evaluating the evidence on which its identification is based. In the present survey the principal name under which a monument is listed is its original Greek name when that has been securely established, in which case its current Turkish name is given second. If the original identification is not secure, it is listed simply under its Turkish name. Since problems of identification are discussed in the introductory texts of each entry, hypothetical identifications can be traced in the index. To alphabetize both Greek and Turkish names in the same list it was necessary to transliterate the Greek names. The Greek names are based on Janin's listings, and Tahsin Öz has been taken as the authority for the Turkish names.[8]

The photographs taken by the author between 1968 and 1973 were made with Pentax 35-mm cameras with lenses of 28, 35, 55, 135, and 200 mm. The author was warned that architectural photography required a larger format negative and perspective-control lenses. But the convenience of the 35-mm camera for work in awkward situations on rooftops or leaning from minarets and its economy in taking multiple exposures were decisive. Perspective-control lenses were avoided for purist aesthetic reasons, for although they succeed in straightening out the perpendicular lines of a composition they do so only at the expense of stretching other parts of the composition. Instead it seemed to preserve the proportions of the architecture more faithfully if a vantage point could be found higher up or further back from which the building could be seen more squarely. In situations in which this was not possible the composition was allowed to stand "uncorrected." For similar reasons artificial light was almost never used.[9] Flash or flood lights cannot be introduced without altering severely the natural lighting of the building, which, it is believed, is as much a part of the architecture as walls or vaults. Interiors were photographed with time exposures. Because of their higher resolution "slow" films were generally used—Agfa IF, Kodak Panotomic X, and Ilford FP4. The laboratory work was done by Ludovico Morelli of Giandean Studio in Rome.

1. Alexander Van Millingen, *Byzantine Churches in Constantinople, Their History and Architecture* (London, 1912).

2. The term "churches," however, has not been extended to include hypogea and simple burial sites. The cisterns sometimes found under churches have also been omitted as belonging rather to civil engineering than church architecture. Within these limits the documentation presented here is complete, as far as the author knows, with the exception of a complex of chapels recently uncovered behind the Istanbul Archaeological Museum, which are still under study by the Museum staff.

3. Raymond Janin, *La géographie ecclésiastique de l'empire byzantin: Constantinople, Les églises et les monastères*. 2nd ed. (Paris, 1969), p. xv.

4. What little remains of Byzantine monuments on the Asiatic shore has been very poorly reported. The relevant bibliography can be found in Jelisaveta S. Allen, ed., *Literature on Byzantine Art*.

1892–1967, Dumbarton Oaks Bibliographies Based on Byzantinische Zeitschrift, series 1 (Washington, D.C., 1973), vol. I, pt. 1, pp. 286–90. On the Princes' Islands the only standing monument is the church of Theotokos Kamariotissa on Heybeliada. Cf. T. Mathews, "Observations on the Church of Panagia Kamariotissa on Heybeliada (Chalke), Istanbul," *DOP* 27 (1973), 115–27. For the ruins of other monuments see R. Janin, "Les Iles des Princes: Étude historique et topographique," *EO* 23 (1924), 178-94.

5. Three plans are presented here that are new. The plan of the Beyazit Churches A, B, and C is drawn from an unpublished plan of Ernest Mamboury in the German Archaeological Institute; the plans of the Kasim Ağa Mescidi and the Toklu Dede Mescidi are based on plans in the Eski Eserleri Koruma Encümeni.

6. Two exceptions are made to this rule, for the Bogdan Sarayı and the Kefeli Mescidi, both of which have their apses to the north.

7. The publication schedule has precluded citing works appearing after 1973.

8. Tahsin Öz, *Istanbul Camileri,* vol. 1 (Ankara, 1962). In transliterating Greek the iota subscript has been omitted.

9. The only exceptions are plates 9-11, 9-13, 9-14, 11-23, and 22-3.

The Churches

1 Hag. Andreas en tē Krisei
2 Atik Mustafa Paşa Camii
3 Aykapı
4 Balaban Ağa Mescidi
5 Beyazit Churches A, B, and C
6 Beyazit Church D
7 Bogdan Sarayı
8 Christos tēs Chōras
9 Christos ho Pantepoptēs
10 Christos ho Pantokratōr
11 Hag. Eirēnē
12 Hag. Euphēmia en tō Hippodromō
13 Gül Camii
14 Hag. Iōannēs Prodromos en tō Hebdomō
15 Hag. Iōannēs Prodromos en tois Stoudiou
16 Hag. Iōannēs Prodromos en tō Troullō
17 Isa Kapısı Mescidi
18 Kalenderhane Camii
19 Kasim Ağa Mescidi
20 Kefeli Mescidi
21 Manastır Mescidi
22 Mangana Churches
23 Hag. Mēnas
24 Myrelaion
25 Odalar Camii
26 Hag. Polyeuktos
27 Sancaktar Hayreddin Mescidi
28 Sekbanbaşı Mescidi
29 Hag. Sergios kai Bakchos en tois Hormisdou
30 Sinan Paşa Mescidi
31 Hagia Sophia
32 Şeyh Murat Mescidi
33 Şeyh Süleyman Mescidi
34 Theotokos tōn Chalkoprateiōn
35 Theotokos tou Libos
36 Theotokos hē Pammakaristos
37 Theotokos hē Panagiotissa
38 Toklu Dede Mescidi
39 Topkapı Sarayı Basilica
40 Vefa Kilise Camii

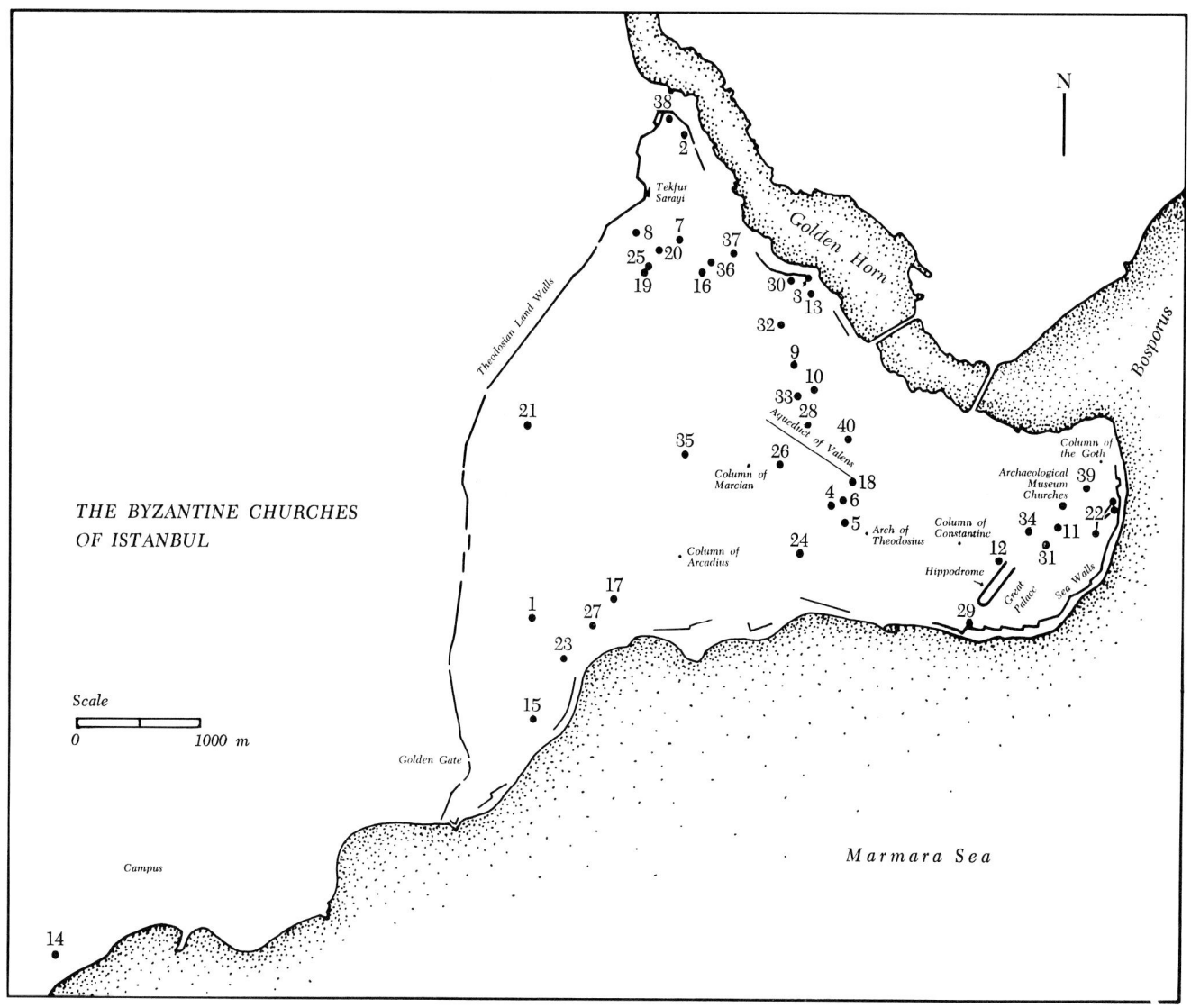

Photo Location Key

View of upper parts of church, galleries, vaulting, or roofs   ⊙10

Ground level or more general view   ⓘ0

View of substructure   10

General view   ⑩—⊣

View of a detail   ⑩⟶

The Churches

1

Hag. Andreas en tē Krisei (St. Andrew at the Place of Judgment). Koca Mustafa Paşa Camii.

The transformation of this church into a mosque in 1489 made of it an archaeological puzzle that has not yet begun to reveal its secrets. The interior was covered with plaster, a portico was added along the north flank, and the exterior was completely refinished in limestone, leaving not a trace of the original masonry visible. Arguments about the primitive shape and date of the monument, therefore, have had to be based on simple observations of the architectural forms. On this basis Ebersolt and Van Millingen, who first surveyed the building, were able to recognize that the main dome is Turkish and that the north and south half-domes below it are revisions of the original design. The rest of the building they assigned to the sixth century, and they reconstructed it as originally an ambulatory church with colonnades north and south of the domed nave, repeating the existing colonnade to the west. According to their reconstruction of the church, the square formed by the four great central arches (still intact) would have towered over the ambulatory zone on three sides while the fourth side opened into the barrel vault of the sanctuary.

This reconstruction seems correct, but the date does not. Eyice's more recent inspection of the building during repairs led him to assign the original fabric to the Palaeologan period instead, specifically to a rebuilding by Theodora Raoulina shortly after 1284. This would make the church nearly contemporary with another ambulatory plan in Istanbul, the south church of Theotokos Lips. In support of Eyice's interpretation one can observe that the narthex design, with its colorful colonnettes against either wall, clearly relates not to Early Byzantine architecture but to the design of the Palaeologan narthex of the Vefa Kilise Camii. Moreover, the chambers that flank the sanctuary at Hag. Andreas are a feature unknown in the early churches of Constantinople.

Eyice's redating of the church, of course, presumes the identification of the building with the church of Hag. Andreas in Byzantine sources; the topographical references are fairly specific, and Janin accepts the identification as beyond question. However, there are references to a church of Hag. Andreas in this vicinity as far back as the eighth century, references which must be interpreted as pertaining to an earlier church. It is possible that some allusion to the early epithet of the monastery, "Rhodophylion," that is, the "rose-petal" monastery, was intended in the rose motif of the Early Byzantine door frame from the site. This deeply undercut frame, now in the garden of the Archaeological Museum, was formerly located in the tekke just west of the church.

The capitals of Hag. Andreas deserve further attention, especially those in the west ambulatory; Kautzsch, in his study of Byzantine capitals, was unwilling to assign them a date. But real progress in understanding the monument can come only through a thorough structural survey and excavation of the site.

Bibliography

Van Millingen, *Byzantine Churches,* pp. 106–21.

Ebersolt and Thiers, *Les églises,* pp. 75–89.

R. Janin, "Les couvents secondaires de Psamathia," *EO* 33 (1933), 326–31.

R. Kautzsch, *Kapitellstudien. Studien zur spätantiken Kunstgeschichte* 9 (Berlin-Leipzig, 1936), pp. 135, 179, 200.

S. Eyice, "Remarques sur deux anciennes églises byzantines d'Istanbul: Koca Mustafa Paşa Camii et l'église de Yuşa tepesi," *Actes du IXe congrès d'études byzantines* (Athens, 1953), 184–90.

Eyice, *Son devir Bizans Mimarisi,* pp. 5–10.

Janin, *La géographie,* pp. 28–31.

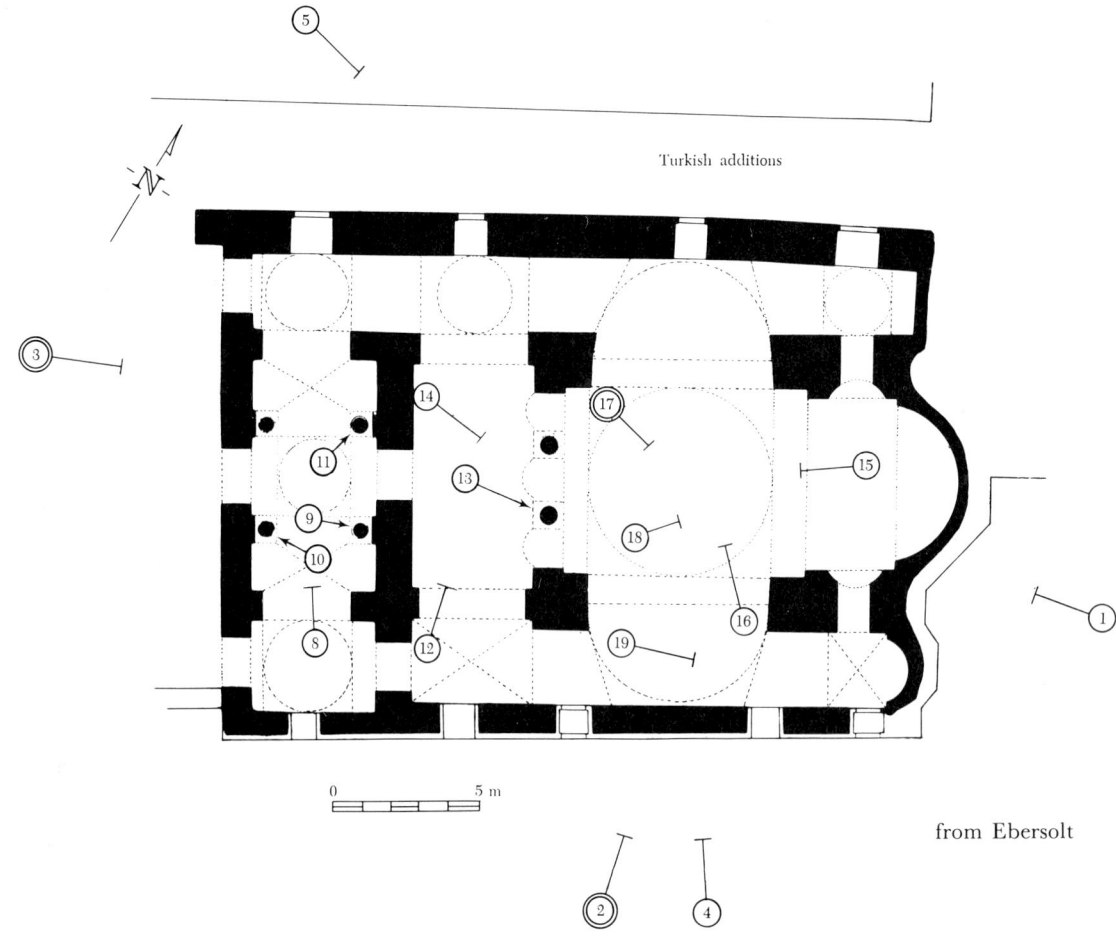

1-1 The east end of the church. M14629

1-2

1-2 Dome and half-domes seen from from the south. M9206
1-3 View from the west above, from the minaret. M21528
1-4 South flank of the church. M14651

6   Hag. Andreas en tē Krisei

1-3

1-4

Hag. Andreas en tē Krisei   7

1-5

1-6

1-7

8 Hag. Andreas en tē Krisei

1-8

1-5 Turkish porch along the north side. M25412
1-6 Door frame, now in the Istanbul Archaeological Museum. M16344
1-7 Detail of door frame. M16346
1-8 Interior of narthex from the south. M15036

1-9

1-10

1-11

1-12

1-13

1-9 Southeast capital in the narthex. M14931
1-10 Southwest capital in the narthex. M14945
1-11 Northeast capital in the narthex. M15114
1-12 West ambulatory from the south. M15032
1-13 South capital in the west ambulatory. M15110

1-14

1-15

1-16

1-14 View from the west ambulatory into the nave. M14915
1-15 Nave, west wall with colonnade. M15014
1-16 Nave, the north apse. M14578

1-17

1-18

1-19

1-17 Dome and half-domes, with the east apse at lower left. M15022
1-18 The sanctuary. M14574
1-19 Right flanking chapel. M14560

2

Atik Mustafa Paşa Camii.   Koca Mustafa Paşa Camii.   Hazreti Cabir Camii.

This mosque, which treasures the remains of the legendary warrior of Islam, Cabir ibn Abdullah, was founded by the same grand vizier, Mustafa Paşa, as was the mosque at Hag. Andreas en tē Krisei. Of the original Byzantine church here, however, neither the name nor the founder is known. Constantius' suggestion of Hag. Petros kai Markos and Eyice's suggestion of Hag. Thekla assume dates in the fifth and twelfth centuries, respectively; and these are too early and too late. From what can be seen of the fabric of the building in its present condition, Van Millingen's date in the ninth century still seems very likely; but serious study of the monument is long overdue. Van Millingen's and Ebersolt's surveys were little more than sketch reports on the building.

On the east end, three broad triple-facet apses of equal height exhibit a bold and rather unusual design that might lend support to the ninth century dating. In the masonry of the side apses one can read a single narrow central window at ground level and three windows higher up, with a diminutive blind niche above the middle window. The central apse, by contrast, has three great, tall windows on the lower level, with three much smaller windows standing almost on the voussoirs of these. The broad brick mullions and simple recessed profiles of the lower windows recall Early Byzantine designs; the massing of the three apses of equal height, however, and the diminutive niches high in the side apses foreshadow the design of the north Lips church (c. 907). The absence of the decorative brickwork that developed rapidly in Middle Byzantine times also suggests that the church belongs to an early stage in the Middle Byzantine development. If further evidence should be found to support a ninth century date, the building would have to be recognized as a key monument in the development of the cross-domed church, a type which Krautheimer and others have regarded as a transitional form between the Early and Middle Byzantine periods. The cross-domed design consists of four converging barrel vaults surmounted by a dome which rests on piers at the crossing.

The dome of the Atik Mustafa Paşa Camii is a Turkish replacement for a dome which must have been higher and windowed. Windows have also been closed up elsewhere in the church, both in the east end and along the flanks; originally, then, the interior was much brighter than it is now. The north and south crossarms opened through triple arcades into porches or aisles. On the south side the Byzantine Institute of America uncovered frescoes of Sts. Michael, Cosmas, and Damian in 1957. Other modern revisions or repairs involved regularizing the roofline on all sides of the building and replacing the narthex with a wooden entrance hall.

Bibliography

Constantius IV, patriarch, *Ancient and Modern Constantinople*, trans. J.P. Brown (London, 1868), p. 83.

Van Millingen, *Byzantine Churches*, pp. 191–95.

Ebersolt and Thiers, *Les églises*, pp. 131–36.

S. Eyice, *Istanbul, Petit guide à travers les monuments byzantins et turcs* (Istanbul, 1955), p. 66.

Krautheimer, *Early Christian and Byzantine Architecture*, pp. 204–11.

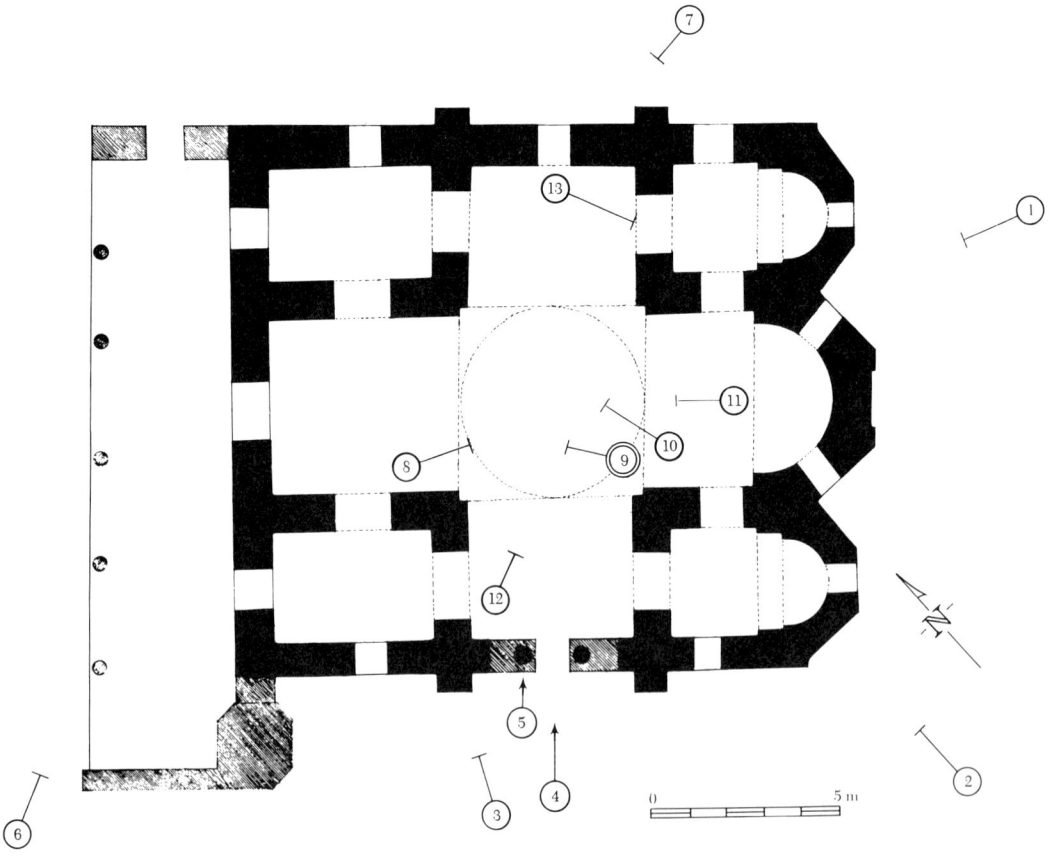

from Ebersolt

2-1 The east end of the church. M8522A

2-2

2-3

2-4

18   Atik Mustafa Paşa Camii

2-2 View from the southeast. M8506
2-3 South flank of the church, detail. M15720
2-4 Arcade in the south flank, with fresco decoration. Dumbarton Oaks Field Committee, H.57.330
2-5 Capital in the south arcade. M5901A
2-6 West façade from the southwest. M7362
2-7 North flank of the church. M8532

Atik Mustafa Paşa Camii

2-8

Atik Mustafa Paşa Camii

2-9

2-8 Interior view toward the sanctuary. M15740
2-9 View of the vaulting, with the west arm of the church below. M15750
2-10 Northwest pier and crossing. M15754

2-10

Atik Mustafa Paşa Camii 21

2-11

2-12

2-13

2-11   West arm of the crossing. M15748
2-12   North arm of the crossing. M15744
2-13   Prothesis chapel. M7335

3

Aykapı Church

This remnant of the substructure of an anonymous chapel shows a masonry similar to that of its neighbor the Gül Camii. The alternating bands of brickwork and stones, with the stones sometimes framed in brick cloisonnés, suggest that the structure should be dated in the eleventh or twelfth century. Schneider's plan and photograph of 1936 are the only existing records of the building, which has since been leveled.

Bibliography

Schneider, *Byzanz*, pp. 53–54.

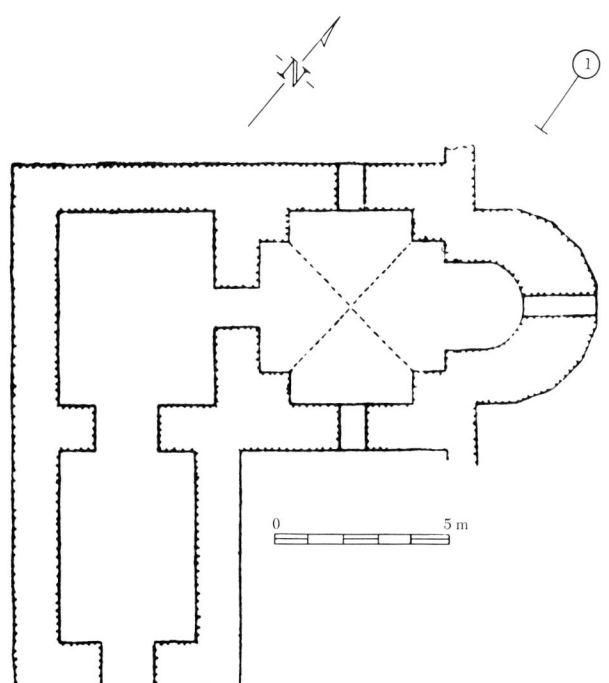

from Schneider

3-1 View from the northeast. A.M. Schneider, German Archaeological Institute in Istanbul, 2696

4

Balaban Ağa Mescidi

Mordtmann's suggestion that this monument be identified as the church of Theotokos tou Kouratoros has never been properly explored. If this hypothesis were confirmed, however, it would give us an important Constantinopolitan martyrium, for the church in question, according to Janin, was established by a government official under Leo I (457–74) in the form of the Holy Sepulchre in Jerusalem, to shelter the relics of Sts. Martha, Mary, and Lazarus. The circular form of the building gives weight to Mordtmann's identification, and so does its location near the ancient Forum Tauri; furthermore, the fifth century date is agreed upon by Van Millingen and Schneider, as well as by the site's excavator, Mansel.

In 1911 Balaban Ağa Mescidi was ravaged by fire, and in 1930 it was sold by the Ministry of Mosques for building material. Virtually nothing was left of it by the time Mansel began his study. The excavation showed that the plan was circular on the exterior but with a flat face on the east and on the west, where the entrance was located before the insertion of the minaret. The interior plan was hexagonal, with a niche on each side and a crypt underneath. In late Byzantine times the crypt was reworked into a square with a domical vault; a burial inscription dated 1345 testifies to the continued use of the crypt in this period. At present, apartments occupy the site of Balaban Ağa Mescidi, and nothing remains of the building.

Bibliography

A.D. Mordtmann, *Equisse topographique de Constantinople* (Lille, 1892), p. 71.

Van Millingen, *Byzantine Churches*, pp. 265–67.

Arif Müfid Mansel, "The Excavation of the Balaban Agha Mesdjidi in Istanbul," *AB* 15 (1933), 210–29.

Schneider, *Byzanz*, 53–55.

R. Janin, "La topographie de Constantinople byzantine: études et découvertes, 1918–38," *EO* 38 (1939), 136.

Janin, *La géographie*, pp. 191–92.

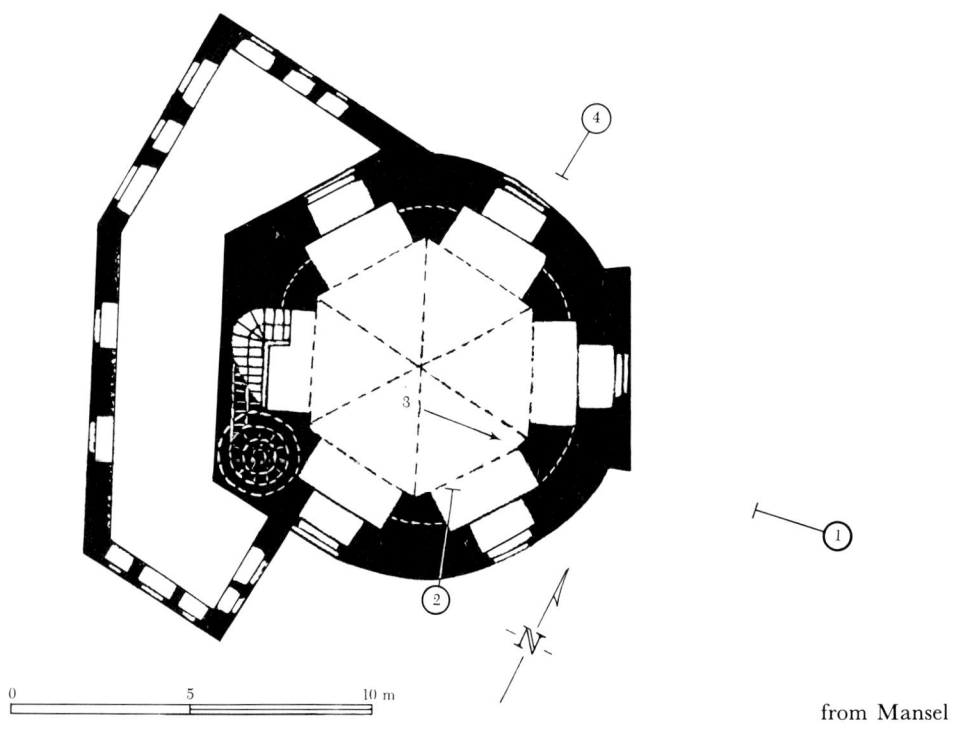

from Mansel

4-1

26 Balaban Ağa Mescidi

4-2

4-3

4-4

4-1 View from the southeast in Paspates' lithograph, 1877
4-2 The excavation seen from the south, with the eastern niche at upper right. Photo Mansel
4-3 Crypt, detail of masonry in the southeast corner. Photo Mansel
4-4 The excavation seen from the north, with the eastern niche at lower left. Photo Mansel

5

Beyazit Churches A, B, and C

The expansion of the University of Istanbul along the Büyük Reşit Paşa Caddesi, which runs up from the site of the ancient Forum Tauri toward the Kalenderhane Camii, has uncovered a succession of four churches, three in 1947 and another (see *Beyazit Church D*) in the winter of 1971–72. This represents an amazing concentration for so short a distance, but unfortunately none of the monuments can be identified. Little was found intact above the foundation level, and the first three churches were destroyed before adequate archaeological soundings were made.

Church A, a basilica, the most important of the first three, seems to be securely dated in the sixth century, as the excavator, Fıratlı, has proposed, not in the fourth, as Mamboury maintained. The site yielded an assortment of architectural sculpture of distinctive Justinianic design, including capitals identical with the nave capitals of Hagia Sophia, which when found carried gold leaf against a blue background. The excavation also turned up the only reasonably complete ambo in Constantinople, a finely carved two-stair ambo in red-veined marble, now reassembled in the garden of Hagia Sophia. The sixth century dating is significant, for no other basilica of the Justinianic period survives in Constantinople. The unusual plan of Church A is discussed in my study of the early churches of the city. The interior dimensions were nearly square; the aisles were segregated from the nave by parapet screens between the columns; open-air courts lay along either side of the building; and an exceptionally wide narthex preceded the entire complex.

Little can be said about Churches B and C except that they, also, were very unusual buildings. The sculptural pieces found here had all been moved before Fıratlı began his survey, and therefore a controlled excavation was not possible. One has little more than the plans to go by, and these are very perplexing.

Church B was found at a level 1.5 meters above Church A, and this, together with its relation to the positions of Churches A and C, seems to indicate that it was built later than the other two, as Fıratlı has suggested. The plan reveals a piscina—perhaps a hagiasma, perhaps a baptismal font—in the center of the nave, and a synthronon in the apse. The multiple subsidiary rooms, symmetrically placed on either side of the church, and the complex entrances to these rooms, seem to defy explanation.

Church C is equally problematical. Schneider speculated that it might have been not a church but a refectory. Fıratlı has proposed a sixth century date for the building, but the scale and plan suggest a later period.

Bibliography

N. Fıratlı, "Découverte de trois églises byzantines à Istanbul," *CA* 5 (1951), 163-78.

E. Mamboury, "Les fouilles byzantines à Istanbul et ses environs," *Byzantion* 21 (1951), 433-37.

A.M. Schneider, Bibliographical note, *BZ* 45 (1952), 222-23.

Mathews, *The Early Churches of Constantinople,* pp. 67-73.

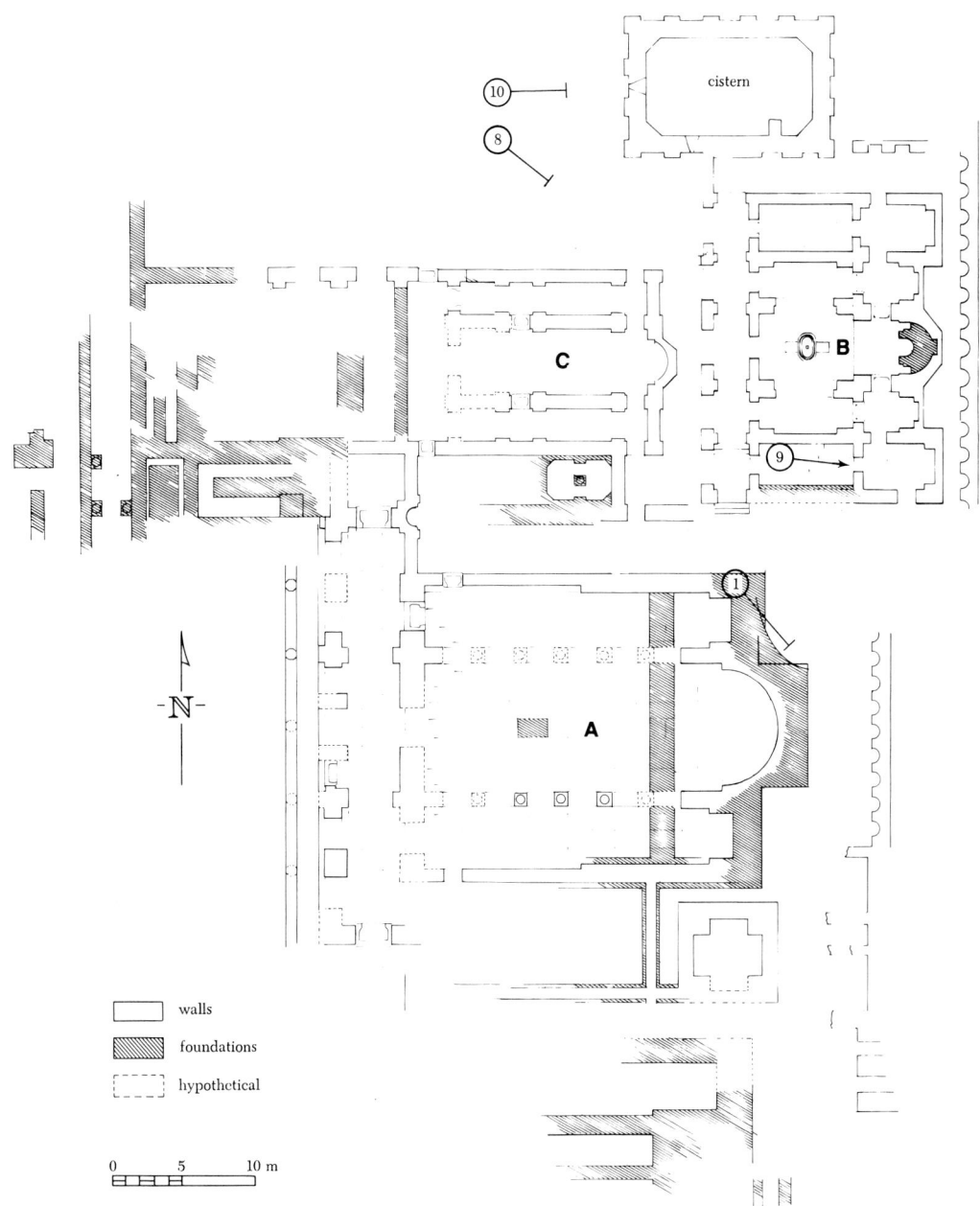

Mathews

5-1

5-1 Church A. Retaining wall. Photo Fıratlı, Eski Eserleri Koruma Encümeni (1947), Istanbul Archaeological Museum

5-2 Church A. Ambo, now in the Hagia Sophia Museum Garden. M18806

5-2

5-3

5-4

5-5

5-6

5-3 Church A. Capital, now in the Hagia Sophia Museum Garden. M612
5-4 Church A. Pilaster capital. Photo Fıratlı, Eski Eserleri Koruma Encümeni (1947), Istanbul Archaeological Museum
5-5 Church A. Capital, now in the Hagia Sophia Museum Garden. M619
5-6 Church A. Cornice fragment. Photo Fıratlı, Eski Eserleri Koruma Encümeni (1947), Istanbul Archaeological Museum

5-7

5-8

32 Beyazit Churches A, B, and C

5-9

5-10

5-11

5-7 Church A. Column base and sculptural fragments. Photo Fıratlı, Eski Eserleri Koruma Encümeni (1947), Istanbul Archaeological Museum
5-8 Church B. General view from the northwest. Photo Fıratlı, Eski Eserleri Koruma Encümeni (1947), Istanbul Archaeological Museum
5-9 Church B. Southeast corner bay from the west. Photo Fıratlı, Eski Eserleri Koruma Encümeni (1947), Istanbul Archaeological Museum
5-10 Church B. Cistern, from the west. Photo Fıratlı, Eski Eserleri Koruma Encümeni (1947), Istanbul Archaeological Museum
5-11 Church B. Fragment of the piscina. Fıratlı, Eski Eserleri Koruma Encümeni (1947), Istanbul Archaeological Museum

6

Beyazit Church D

The fourth church was found in 1971, during excavations for university expansion, to the north of the other three, just south of the intersection of Büyük Reşit Paşa Caddesi and Vezneciler Caddesi. Except for a few courses of rising wall in the east end, only the massive concrete foundations remained.

    The site has not yet been published, but it has been surveyed by Fıratlı and Striker, and pottery finds made by Striker in the undisturbed soil under the foundations date the church firmly in the late eleventh century. The plan of the foundations shows many irregularities, but the rising walls might have been more carefully laid out. It is probable that Church D was a cross-domed type of structure, for there does not appear to be room to fit the eastern corner bays of a quincunx design on the present foundations. The masonry is of regular brick courses lightly plastered over and roughly stroked to imitate stone courses. On completion of the Fıratlı and Striker study of the building, the remains are to be destroyed for a new building site.

6-1

6-2

6-1 General view of the site from the north. M26604
6-2 General view from the east, showing the apses rising from the broad foundation. M26617

7

Bogdan Sarayı

This little single-naved chapel belongs to a group of three monuments in the same area (the Odalar Camii and the Kefeli Mescidi are the others) whose Byzantine history is unknown but whose Christian use in Turkish times is fairly well documented. In the early sixteenth century the church became part of the residence of the Rumanian embassy to the Sublime Porte and was known as Hag. Nikolaos. In 1760 it was attached to the monastery of Panteleimon on Mount Athos, but after devastation in the fire of 1784 it was abandoned, and has since gradually fallen into ruin.

When Van Millingen surveyed the monument—then in use as a barn—two stories of it were still intact, and in places as many as four layers of fresco covered the interior walls. Van Millingen noticed evidence that the building had originally been attached to other structures on the east (the apse points to the north). He also observed that the church's blind dome represented a second building phase, having replaced an earlier timber roof.

A note by Papadopulos reports that the Germans excavated the lower church during World War I, discovering an inscription and three sarcophagi; these findings, however, were lost without being recorded. At present the lower story, which serves as a dwelling, is all that remains of Bogdan Sarayī. Because of the alternation of brick and stone voussoirs in the arch of the south entrance, and the articulation of the apse at the opposite end of the building, Eyice's Palaeologan dating seems preferable to the twelfth century hypothesis of Van Millingen.

Bibliography

Van Millingen, *Byzantine Churches,* pp. 280–87.

M. Papadopulos, "Note sur quelques découvertes récentes faites à Constantinople," *Académie des inscriptions et belles-lettres, Comptes rendus* (1920), 63.

Eyice, *Son devir Bizans Mimarisi,* pp. 32–34.

Janin, *La géographie,* p. 371.

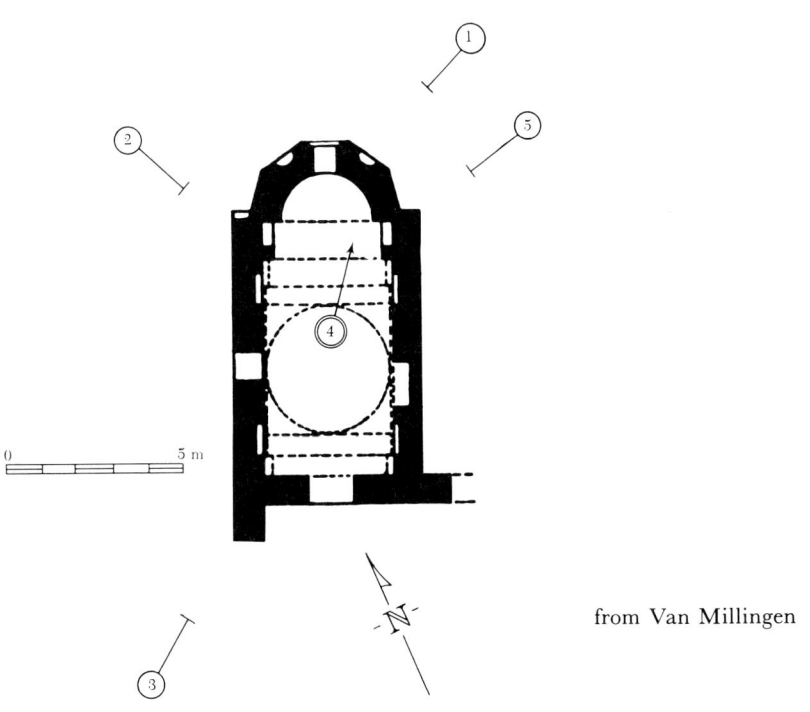

from Van Millingen

7-1 View from the northeast in Paspates' lithograph, 1877

Bogdan Sarayı

7-2

38 Bogdan Sarayı

7-3

7-4

7-5

7-2 General view from the northwest, c. 1910. Photo Van Millingen, courtesy Burrows Library of Byzantine and Modern Greek, King's College, University of London

7-3 Lower story from the south, c. 1925. Photo A.K. Porter Collection, neg. 5424, courtesy Fogg Art Museum, Harvard University

7-4 Interior, detail of apse vaulting, c. 1910. Photo Van Millingen, courtesy Burrows Library of Byzantine and Modern Greek, King's College, University of London

7-5 Present state of the monument, from the east. M21302

8

Christos tēs Chōras (Christ of the Chōra).
Ka'riye Camii.

The credit for this extraordinary building and its lavish mosaic and fresco decoration belongs to the statesman and poet Theodore Metochites, who made of it one of Byzantine civilization's most important monuments. No other church of Constantinople can boast so extensive a decorative program, and no other, outside of Hagia Sophia, is as well known.

A little more than a century ago, however, the monument was still unrecognized, having been in use as a mosque since the time of Beyazit II. It was only after 1860, following its rediscovery and its subsequent cleaning by the Turkish government, that the mosaics were gradually revealed. Inscriptions which accord Christ and the Virgin the mystical title Chōra, meaning "the dwelling place," established the church's identity, and an extensive bibliography of comment quickly grew up around the monument.

In 1948 a second, more extensive undertaking of cleaning and restoration was begun. Under the sponsorship of the Byzantine Institute of America and the Dumbarton Oaks Center for Byzantine Studies, Thomas Whittemore organized the project to clean and consolidate all the mosaics and to uncover the frescoes of the parekklesion, which were still concealed by whitewash. The work was directed by Ernest Hawkins and took eleven years. The entire decorative program was subsequently published by Underwood in a monumental three-volume descriptive study, with a fourth volume of commentary still in preparation.

The Whittemore-Underwood project also included a limited excavation to unravel the complex architectural history of the monument. In general, however, less attention has been given to structural analysis of the building than it deserves, the architecture having been overshadowed by the exceptional interest of the decoration. To early scholars of the building, both its long and distinguished history and the very unusual, asymmetrical layout posed considerable problems. Shmit, whose great two-volume work remained the standard monograph on the church for sixty years, reconstructed the original core of the building along the lines of the Koimēsis of Nicaea and estimated its date as the seventh century. Rüdell proposed a similar solution; his analysis of the structure was more thorough than Shmit's and is in many ways more complete than Underwood's, even though it was made without the benefit of the latter's excavation. A shorter account of the church was also prepared by Van Millingen, who, like Shmit and Rüdell, attempted to piece together an Early Byzantine plan for the building. As the Whittemore excavation eventually demonstrated, however, nothing in the present church can be dated earlier than the Comnenian period; only under the east end of the building are there any elements of earlier substructures.

The excavation results, first reported by Oates and later recapitulated in Underwood's publication, distinguished two phases within the Comnenian era, both marked by the characteristic recessed brick masonry of the time. Of the former phase only foundations remained, indicating a small quincunx plan whose total width corresponded to the width of the present nave. This building, which Underwood attributes to Maria Ducaena, 1077–81, was razed to make way for a second building, the core of which constitutes the central unit of the present church—the broad apse and domed square nave, which are datable to Isaac Comnenus, c. 1120. The narthex and side chapels of this second building, however, were in turn replaced by the extensive rebuilding campaign of Metochites between 1315 and 1321, which gave the structure its present shape.

On first entering Metochites' church one finds an outer narthex that runs across the entire west façade. Decorated with mosaics of the life of Christ, this space was once much brighter than at present, more like an open porch; the large window bays across the façade were closed up by the Turks. On the main axis of the church one then enters the more confining inner narthex, lighted only by the broken rays entering the drums of the two cupolas. This space, glistening with colorful marble revetments, is dedicated to the life of the Virgin and dominated by the grand mosaic of her intercession with Christ. One then proceeds to the Comnenian nave, an airy open space under the broad cupola. Metochites found it necessary to rebuild the drum in his day, but whatever decoration he put there was destroyed when the dome collapsed in Turkish times. To the north of the nave Metochites added a two-storied, barrel-vaulted annex of possible monastic purpose, and to the south he built the chief object of his entire reconstruction program—a delicately designed mortuary chapel, frescoed with promises of the Resurrection. Here burial places were provided in niches beneath carved arches. Recently both the Palaeologan and Comnenian sculpture in the church have been studied by Wessel and Belting, respectively.

In the post-Byzantine era, some alterations have been made in the exterior appearance of the Chōra, similar to those made on other Byzantine monuments in Istanbul. In this instance, the undulating rooflines have been brought up to a firm horizontal, and the gentle, scalloped profile of the drums has given way to a heavier, helmeted appearance. A minaret was placed at the southwest corner where once a belfry might have stood.

Bibliography

F.I. Shmit, *Kakhrie-Dzami*, Izvestiia Russkago Arkheologischeskago Instituta v Konstantinople, 11 (Sofia and Munich, 1906).

A. Rüdell, *Die Kahrie-Dschamisi in Constantinopel, ein Kleinod byzantinischer Kunst* (Berlin, 1908).

Van Millingen, *Byzantine Churches*, pp. 288–331.

D. Oates, "A Summary Report on the Excavations of the Byzantine Institute in the Kariye Camii, 1957–58," *DOP* 14 (1960), 223–31.

P.A. Underwood, *The Kariye Djami*, Bollingen Series 70, 3 vols. (New York, 1966).

Janin, *La géographie*, pp. 531–38.

K. Wessel, "Byzantinische Plastik der palaiologischen Periode," *Byzantion* 36 (1966), 217–59.

H. Belting, "Ein Gruppe Konstantinopler Reliefs aus dem 11. Jahrhundert," *Pantheon* 30, 4 (1972), 263–71.

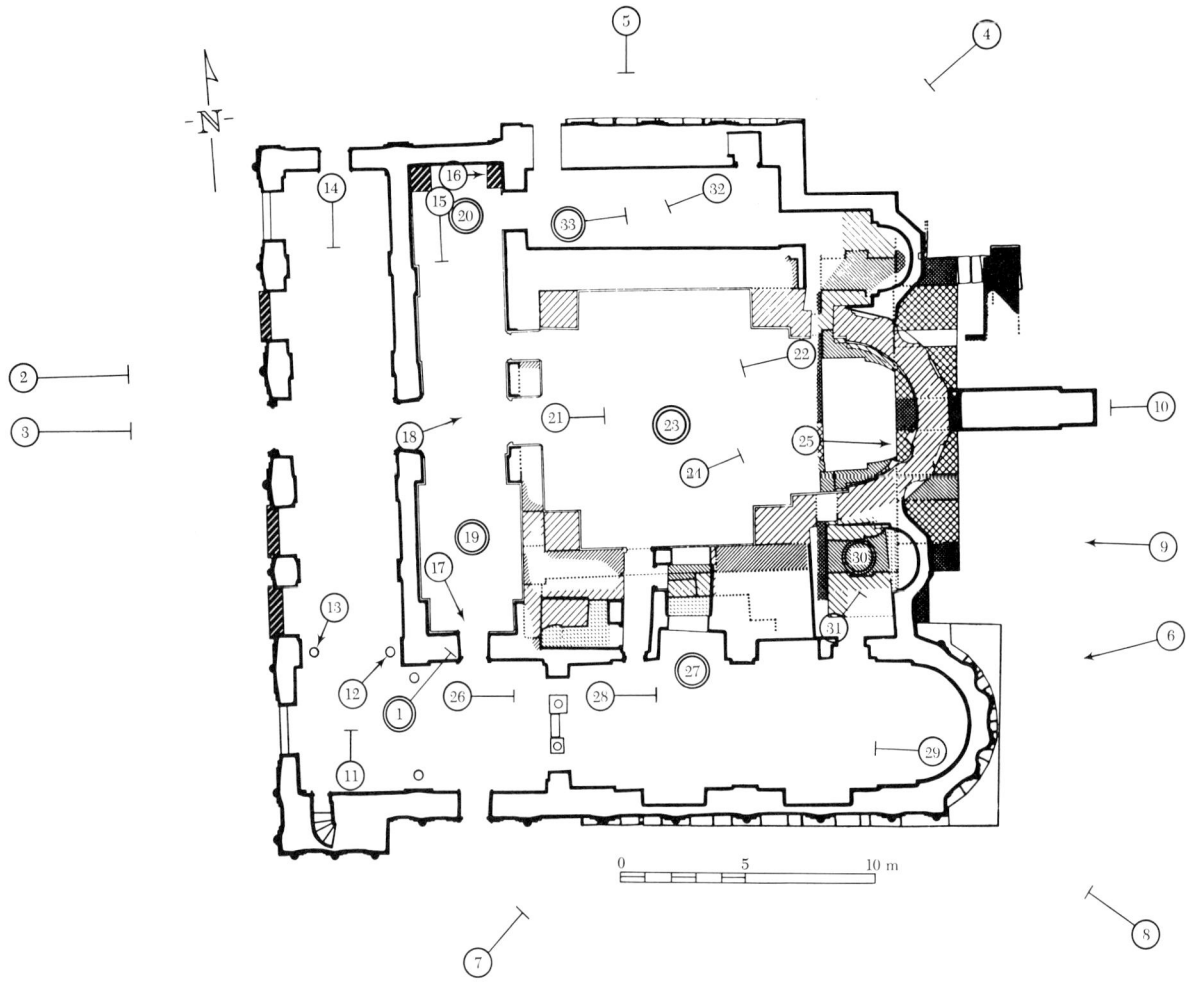

from Underwood

8-1 General view of the main church from above, from the minaret. M16522

8-2

8-3

44   Christos tēs Chōras

8-4

8-2 View from the west in Paspates' lithograph, 1877
8-3 View from the west. M19502
8-4 General view from the northeast. M15158
8-5 North annex from the north. M15174

8-5

Christos tēs Chōras 45

8-6

8-7

8-8

8-6 Parekklesion apse. M15148
8-7 South flank of the parekklesion. M19315
8-8 General view of the main church and parekklesion from the southeast. M19405

8-9

8-10

8-9 Side chapel between the parekklesion and the main sanctuary, built on the remains of earlier structures. M15150
8-10 Main apse. M15152
8-11 Outer narthex, viewed from the south end. M24614A

8-11

8-12

8-13

8-12 Capital in the outer narthex, at the northeast corner of the south bay. M11009
8-13 Capital in the outer narthex, at the northwest corner of the south bay. M11015
8-14 Outer narthex, viewed from the north end. M24607
8-15 Inner narthex, viewed from the north. M24603A
8-16 Inner narthex, sculptural detail in the arcosolium at the north end. M11033

8-14

8-15

8-16

8-17

8-18

8-17 Inner narthex, doorway to the parekklesion. M11204A
8-18 Doorway from the inner narthex to the nave. M11136
8-19 Inner narthex, south cupola, with the north below. Photo Byzantine Institute, Dumbarton Oaks, K602-53-30
8-20 Inner narthex, north cupola, with the east below. Photo Byzantine Institute, Dumbarton Oaks, K602-58-156

8-19

8-20

8-21

8-22

8-21 The nave and sanctuary as seen in 1909. Photo Sir I. Benjamin Stone, courtesy the Reference Library of the Birmingham Public Libraries, England
8-22 The nave viewed from the east. M10917A
8-23 The vaulting of the nave and sanctuary. M24507
8-24 The sanctuary. M24501
8-25 Inlaid decoration in a spandrel of the sanctuary window. M11022

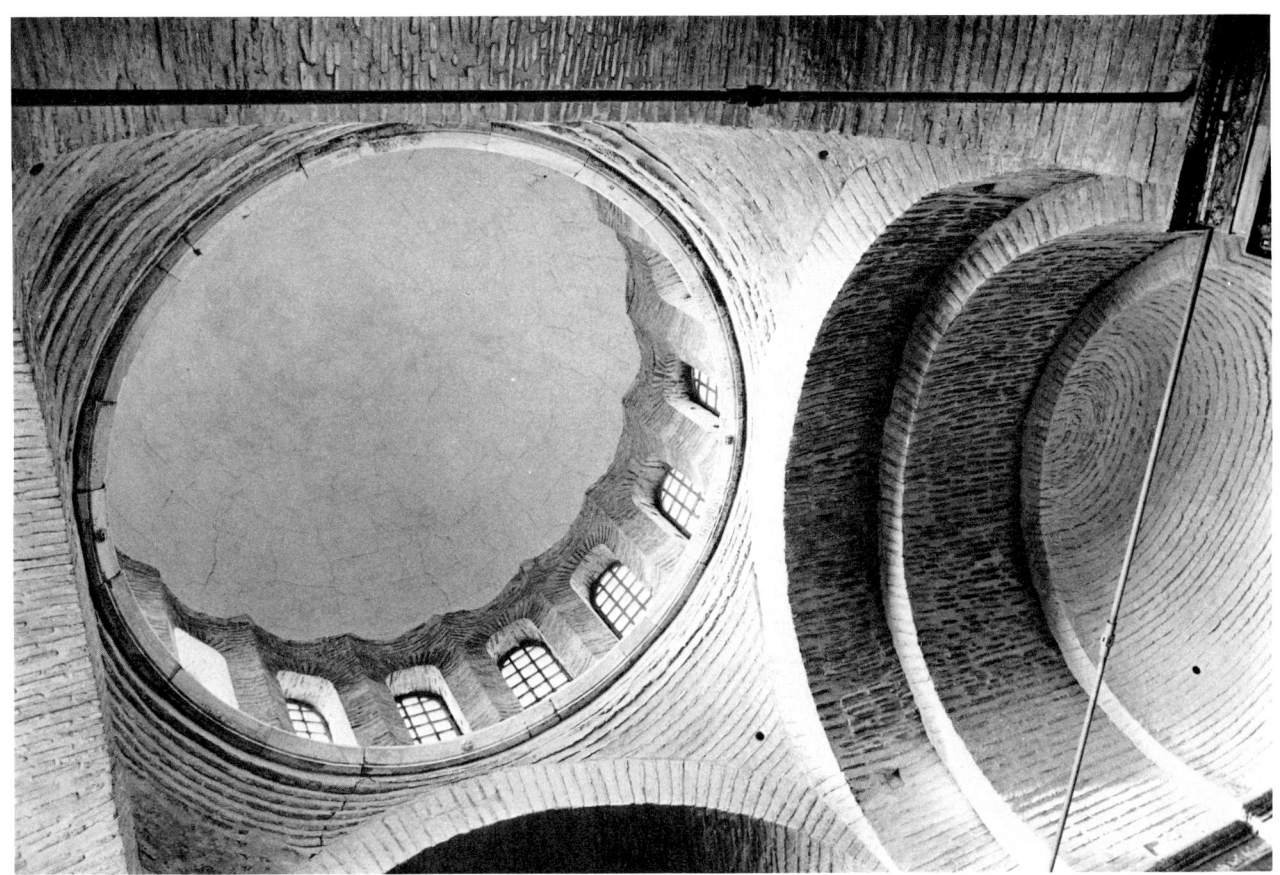

8-23

8-24

8-25

Christos tēs Chōras

8-26

8-27

8-28

8-29

8-26 Parekklesion, general view from the west. M15252
8-27 Parekklesion, view into the cupola. M24620A
8-28 The east end of the parekklesion. M15264
8-29 The west end of the parekklesion. M15274

8-30

8-31

8-32

8-33

8-30 Cupola of the side chapel between the parekklesion and the main sanctuary. M16457
8-31 Side chapel between the parekklesion and the main sanctuary. M16449
8-32 North annex viewed toward the west. M16465
8-33 Gallery of the north annex, viewed toward the east. M16429

9

Christos ho Pantepoptēs (Christ the All-Seeing).
Eski Imaret Camii.

Judged by Van Millingen to be "the most carefully built of the later churches of Constantinople," the church of the Pantepoptēs is also one of the least studied Byzantine monuments of the city. Apart from Van Millingen's and Ebersolt's surveys, no literature of any importance exists on it; moreover, the structure has rarely been photographed. Located in one of the poorer sections of Istanbul, it is closely hemmed in on all sides, making an adequate view difficult, and its present use as an Islamic theological school also renders it somewhat inaccessible for scientific study. Yet it is the only documented eleventh century church in Istanbul that has survived intact, and it is a key monument of Middle Byzantine architecture.

Anna Dalassena, mother of Alexius I, erected the church sometime before 1087 and later retired to apartments in the monastery there, as Janin relates. It was possibly for her private use that the church's unique U-shaped gallery was designed, extending over the narthex and over the two western corner bays of the quincunx plan, with interior windows opening onto both the nave and the crossarms. This clever interlocking of gallery and quincunx results in the regular, cubical massing of the exterior of the church. The exterior is noteworthy as well for its decorative niches above the window zone of the main apse, and for the regular use of recessed brick enlivened by occasional decorative motifs—sunbursts, meanders, basket-weave patterns, and cloisonnés.

Along the north side of the church, Van Millingen and Constantius both reported evidence of abutting monastic structures, but this side is now concealed by dwellings built immediately adjacent to it. Brunov's hypothesis, meanwhile, suggesting that additional aisles originally flanked the church for the use of choirs during the liturgy seems to be incorrect; this suggestion is unsupported by any liturgical documents, and is also irreconcilable with the design of the south side of the building. The outer narthex of Pantepoptēs appears to be an addition of the Palaeologan period.

Of the original interior decoration, all that remain are a few fine, sculptured cornices and door frames. In Turkish times the four columns that formerly supported the crossing were replaced with piers, and the colonnades at either end of the crossarms were filled in. The triple window of the sanctuary was also revised to a single opening, and the apses flanking the sanctuary were resurfaced. The Turks also built a minaret at the building's southwest corner, but only its foundation remains.

Now, after periods of relative neglect, the Ministry of Mosques is restoring the structure. The project has returned the dome to its original scalloped roofline, and has replaced the tentlike roofing of the gallery with tiles that follow the gentle curves of the vaulting. The masonry, however, is being repointed in a way that threatens to destroy all evidence of the original surface.

Bibliography

Constantius IV, patriarch, *Constantiniade ou description de Constantinople ancienne et moderne,* trans. M.R. (Constantinople, 1846), p. 108.

Van Millingen, *Byzantine Churches,* pp. 212–18.

Ebersolt and Thiers, *Les églises,* pp. 171–82.

N. Brunov, "Über zwei byzantinische Baudenkmäler von Konstantinopel aus dem XI Jahrhundert," *Byzantinisch-Neugriechische Jahrbücher* 9 (1931–32), 129–44.

Janin, *La géographie,* pp. 513–15.

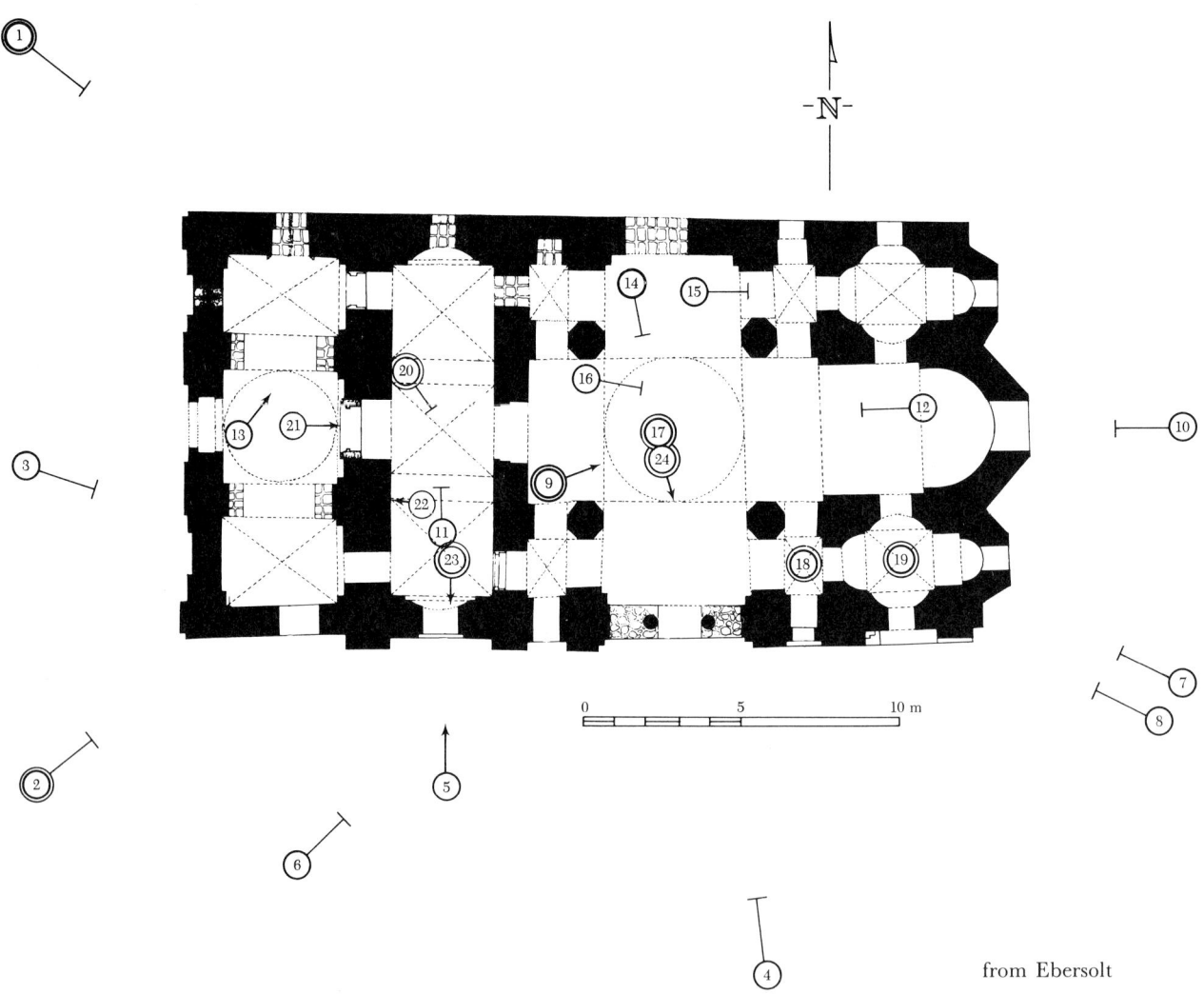

from Ebersolt

9-1

9-2

9-1 General view from the northwest. M27424
9-2 General view from the southwest before the restoration. M21146

9-3

9-4

9-5

9-3 The west façade c. 1940. Photo Artamonoff, courtesy the Dumbarton Oaks Field Committee.
9-4 The south flank of the church. M26313
9-5 The south flank before restoration, detail of the inner narthex and gallery bay. M17964
9-6 The south flank before restoration. M17956

9-6

9-7

9-8

9-7 General view from the southeast in 1940. Eski Eserleri Koruma Encümeni, 3579, Istanbul Archaeological Museum
9-8 General view from the southeast at present. M26306
9-9 The cupola before restoration, as seen from the southwest. M21111
9-10 General view from the east. M21054

9-9

9-10

9-11

9-11 The inner narthex, viewed from the south. M11803
9-12 General view of the interior from the sanctuary. M27515

9-12

9-13

9-14

9-15

9-16

9-13 The outer narthex, north end. M11809
9-14 The south arm of the crossing. M11716
9-15 The prothesis chapel. M8624
9-16 The sanctuary. M27510

9-17

9-18

9-19

9-17 The dome and pendentives, with the east side below. M11722
9-18 The vaulting of the southeast corner bay. M11736
9-19 The vaulting of the diaconicon chapel. M11731

9-20

9-21

9-22

9-24

9-23

9-20 The gallery, viewed from the north. A.K. Porter Collection, 1248, courtesy the Fogg Art Museum, Harvard University

9-21 Lintel over the center door leading from the outer to the inner narthex, c. 1935. Photo Sender, rephotographed

9-22 Detail of the cornice in the inner narthex. M8808

9-23 Detail of the cornice in the gallery. Photo Sender, rephotographed

9-24 Detail of the cornice in the drum. A.K. Porter Collection, 1250, courtesy the Fogg Art Museum, Harvard University

10

Christos ho Pantokratōr, Theotokos hē Eleousa, and Hag. Michaēl (Christ the All-Ruler, the Mother-of-God the Merciful, and Saint Michael). Zeyrek Camii.

The great triple church of Christos Pantokratōr, standing on the brow of the fourth hill of the city, is the largest and most important Middle Byzantine foundation of Constantinople. Its prominence in Byzantine history as the burial place of the Comnenian dynasty and its conspicuous situation high above the Golden Horn have always assured its proper identification, even though the structure was converted to a mosque by Mehmet the Conqueror.

Perhaps on the initiative of his wife, Irene, the church complex was built by John II Comnenus between 1118, the year of his accession, and 1136, the date of the Typicon he drew up to govern the monastery to which the churches were attached. The Typicon, which has been published by Dmitrievskij and summarized by both Hergès and Janin, is an extremely important source that deserves to be better known; it not only details all the workings of the Pantokratōr and a hospital that was affiliated with it, but it sets forth the order of ceremonies to be celebrated in the churches, with important, concrete information on the inner life and original appearance of these monuments. The architecture itself also merits much more attention than it has received. Though Megaw has added considerably to our knowledge of the south church, Van Millingen's and Ebersolt's surveys are all that we have on the total complex.

The problem of the building sequence, puzzled over by earlier authors, has found its solution in Megaw's study of the seams and joints between the buildings, and this is confirmed by the data in the Typicon. The double-narthexed south church, dedicated to the Pantokratōr, was the first to be erected; it was soon followed by the north church, dedicated to Theotokos hē Eleousa, where every Friday the icon of the Hodēgētria was brought from the imperial palace for solemn veneration. Last came the central church, the heroon or mausoleum, dedicated to Hag. Michaēl; its confined location explains some of the irregularities of its unique, two-domed plan.

Megaw has also clarified the building phases of the south church. The outer narthex was added, he concluded, after the church was completed, and at that time the vaulting of the middle bay in the inner narthex was cut through and a cupola was added above the gallery to provide a funnel of light to the inner narthex. South of the diaconicon Megaw reported two groin-vaulted bays, omitted in previous plans, which appear to be the remains of an original south aisle. Outside the building to the south are further ruins, remains of the monastery, which have yet to be properly studied. Of the interior decoration of this church, some signs are still present to confirm its original elegance: the rose marble door frames of the narthex, the fine revetment in the apse, and the sumptuous inlaid marble pavement uncovered by the Byzantine Institute of the United States and reported by Schweinfurth and Underwood. Fragments of stained glass which were found here by Megaw have been discussed by Lafond.

In the north church, some overzealous restoration by the Ministry of Mosques has destroyed much evidence, especially in the west façade, and it is not clear whether the present cupola is Byzantine or Turkish. But the fine sculptural decoration of the building's interior, hitherto unpublished, has survived and deserves special notice. By contrast with the fragile intricacies of the tenth century Lips church, the other most important example of Middle Byzantine sculptural decoration, the gallery capitals and gallery-level cornice of the Eleousa exhibit a vigorous and broadly worked style. On the cornice, which was probably painted originally, a vine with pomegranates is used to enframe a variety of motifs including chalices, peacocks, formalized leaves, cocks fighting, doves adossed at a tree-of-life, and various birds of the hunt.

Hag. Michaēl, the central church of the complex, served as the imperial mausoleum under the Comnenes; at present it is in use as a mosque. The spacious interior of this curious, single-apsed, double-domed structure is now whitewashed and empty of the imperial sarcophagi it once held. Mango has discovered both archaeological and epigraphical evidence of one of the tombs, that of Manuel I, which stood in the entranceway leading from the south church; a second of the Comnene tombs is presently in the Hagia Sophia Museum.

In modern times the exteriors of all three churches have been mutilated on the east end by window revisions. Higher up, however, the tall, elegant niches and decorative brickwork that graced the structures are still intact. Inside the buildings, no major changes have been made apart from the loss of original wall decoration and the replacement of all columns by modern piers.

Bibliography

A. Dmitrievskij, *Opisanie Liturgičeskike Rukopisei*, I *Typica* (Kiev, 1895), pp. 656–702.

A. Hergès, "Le monastère du Pantocrator à Constantinople," *EO* 2 (1898–99), 70–88.

Van Millingen, *Byzantine Churches*, pp. 219–42.

Ebersolt and Thiers, *Les églises*, pp. 185–207.

P. Schweinfurth, "Der Mosaikfussboden der Komnenischen Pantokratorkirche in Istanbul," *Jahrbüch des Deutschen Archäologischen Instituts* 69 (1954), 253–60.

P.A. Underwood, "Notes on the Work of the Byzantine Institute in Istanbul: 1954," *DOP* 9–10 (1956), 299–300.

A.H.S. Megaw, "Notes on Recent Work of the Byzantine Institute in Istanbul," *DOP* 17 (1963), 335–64.

J. Lafond, "Les vitraux historiés du moyen âge découverts récemment à Constantinople," *Bull. Soc. Nat. Antiquaires de France* (1964), 164–66.

C. Mango, "Notes on Byzantine Monuments: Tomb of Manuel I Comnenus," *DOP* 23–24 (1969–70), 372–75.

Janin, *La géographic,* pp. 175–76, 344, 515–23.

10-1 General view from the west. M26013

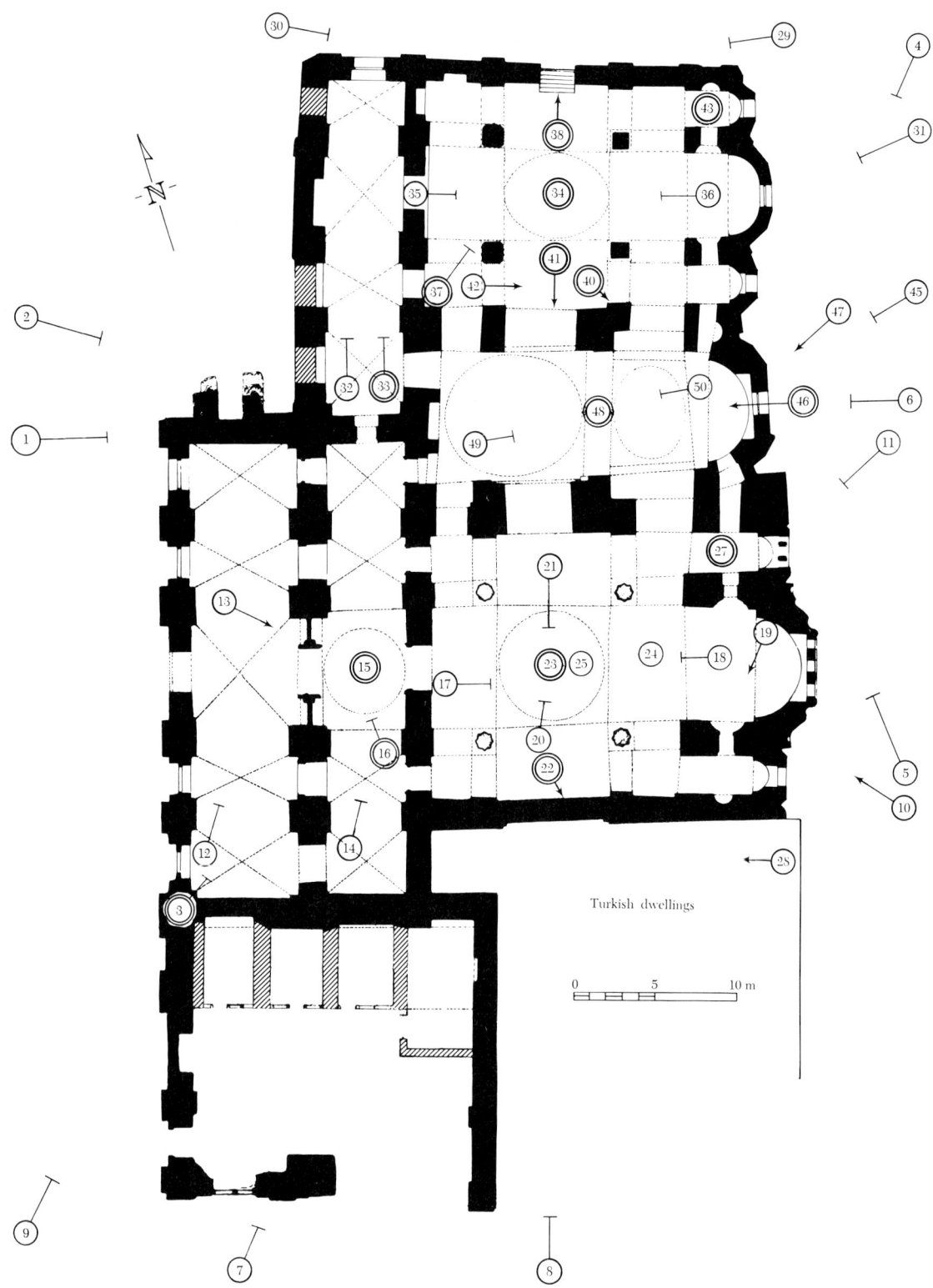

10-2

10-3

10-2 General view from the west. M21119
10-3 General view from above, from the minaret. M11529A

Christos ho Pantokratōr 75

10-4

10-4 General view from the east. M17649
10-5 The apses from the southeast. M27127

10-5

10-6

10-7

10-6 General view from the east. M11506A

10-7 South church, general view from the southwest. A.K. Porter Collection, 5343, courtesy the Fogg Art Museum, Harvard University

10-8

10-9

10-8 South church, the south flank. M27101A
10-9 South church, the façade seen from the southwest. M10237

10-10

80   Christos ho Pantokratōr

10-11

10-12

10-10 South church, detail of the articulation of the east end. M27208
10-11 South church, the east end seen from the northeast. M26406
10-12 South church, the outer narthex viewed from the south. M6224
10-13 South church, marble door frames between the outer and inner nartheces. M6231

10-13

10-14

10-15

10-14 South church, the inner narthex viewed from the south. M6235
10-15 South church, cupola over the inner narthex gallery, with the east at the right. M7913
10-16 South church, gallery over the inner narthex, viewed from the south. M7905

10-16

Christos ho Pantokratōr   83

10-17

10-17 South church, the sanctuary. M11304
10-18 South church, general interior view from the sanctuary. M11335

10-18

10-19

10-20

10-21

10-22

86   Christos ho Pantokratōr

10-23

10-19 South church, detail of the marble revetment in the sanctuary. M11318
10-20 South church, north crossarm. M6120A
10-21 South church, south crossarm. M6112A
10-22 South church, window capital in the south crossarm. M7935
10-23 South church, cupola and vaulting, with the east below. M6123A

10-24

10-24 South church, detail of the pavement showing Samson slaying the Philistines. M6209
10-25 South church, overall view of the pavement from the west. Dumbarton Oaks Field Committee, 61.172
10-26 South church, templon parapet, spoiled from the sixth century Hag. Polyeuktos. M6218

10-25

10-26

Christos ho Pantokratōr 89

10-27

10-28

10-27 South church, vaulting of the prothesis chapel. M6131A
10-28 South church, remains of an aisle south of the church, from the east. M27118
10-29 North church, viewed from the northeast. M17660
10-30 North church, the north flank from the northwest. M17711

10-29

10-30

10-31   North church, viewed from the east. M26435

10-32

10-32 North church, the narthex viewed from the south. M6233
10-33 North church, the narthex gallery viewed from the south. M7772
10-34 North church, the vaulting of the cupola and crossarms, with the east below. M27035
10-35 North church, general interior view from the west. M11423A

10-33

92   Christos ho Pantokratōr

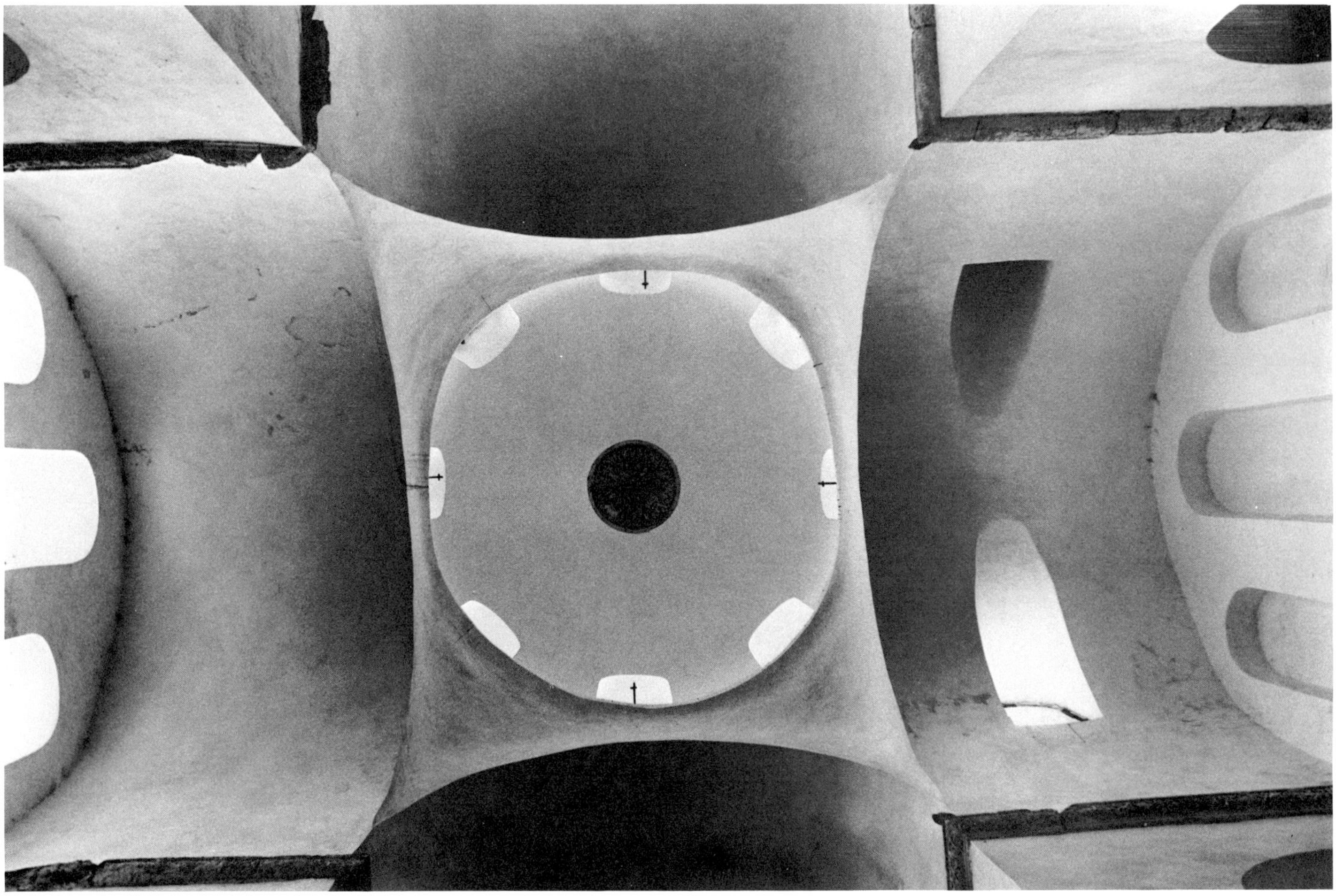

10-34

10-35

Christos ho Pantokratōr 93

10-36

10-37

10-38

10-36   North church, general interior view from the sanctuary. M27015
10-37   North church, view of the north wall and vaulting. M5404A
10-38   North church, mosaic remains in the soffit of the window in the north wall. M17804

10-39

10-40

10-41

96   Christos ho Pantokratōr

10-42

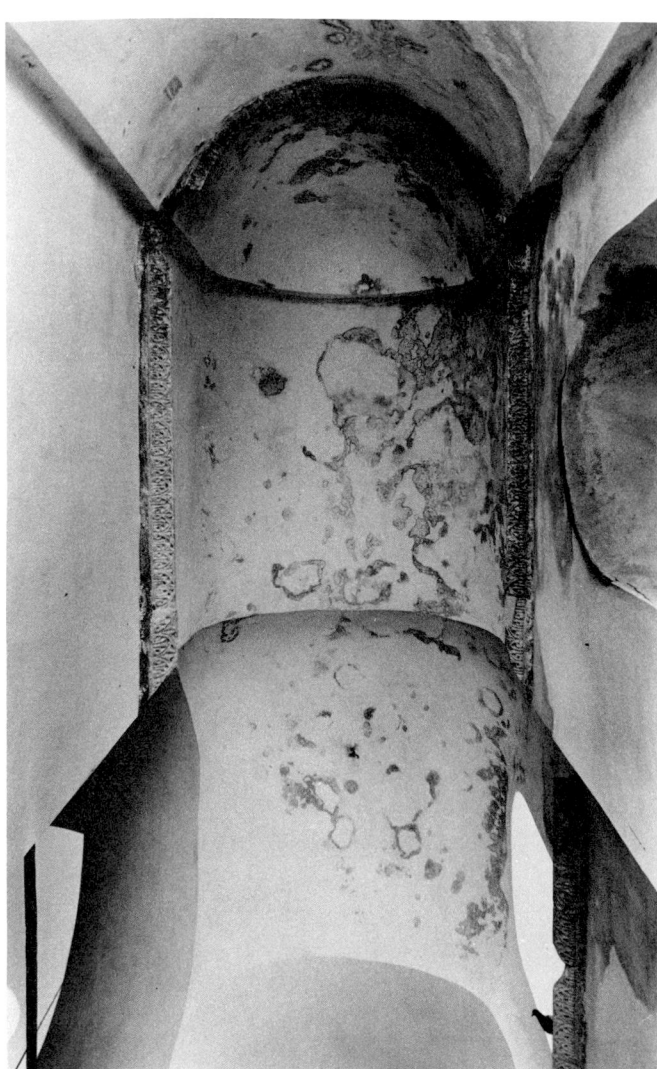

10-43

10-44

10-39 North church, detail of the window capital from the narthex gallery. M7818
10-40 North church, detail of the gallery-level cornice in the south crossarm. M26811
10-41 North church, detail of the gallery-level cornice in the south crossarm. M26804
10-42 North church, the south aisle and diaconicon chapel. M7810
10-43 North church, the vaulting in the diaconicon chapel. M27030
10-44 North church, fragments from the gallery-level cornice. M26820

10-45

98 Christos ho Pantokratōr

10-46

10-47

10-45   Middle church, general view from the northeast. M26404
10-46   Middle church, the eastern dome seen from the east. M26432
10-47   Middle church, detail of the niches in the apse. M26416

Christos ho Pantokratōr   99

10-48

100   Christos ho Pantokratōr

10-49

10-50

10-48 Middle church, the vaulting, with the east dome at the right. M11230A
10-49 Middle church, the interior, from the west. M5435
10-50 Middle church, the interior, from the east. M11223A

11

Hag. Eirēnē (Holy Peace)

Except for its neighbor Hag. Sophia, just 110 meters to the south, the church of Hag. Eirēnē carries the largest dome of Byzantine architecture, spanning a full 16 meters and soaring to an apex almost 35 meters above the floor. When viewed from the outside, the grandeur of these dimensions is now somewhat diminished by a rise in the ground level of up to 5 meters; inside, however, the full effect is still felt with great force. Four massive barrel vaults lift the dome's pendentives far above the nave, and this central domed unit combines with a great synthronon-banked apse on the east and a sail-vaulted bay on the west to form a huge, uninterrupted interior space. The entire area is embraced by broad aisles and galleries in a U shape, including the narthex. To the west lies an atrium, formerly a large, open space which has been reduced in Turkish times by the insertion of new porticoes on all four sides.

Hag. Eirēnē was never a mosque, and its Byzantine past, which is ably summarized by Janin, has always been well known. The chief problem of scholarship on the church has always been that of matching the archaeological evidence with the sketchy framework provided by historical sources. We know that the present building's first phase dates from 532, when Justinian decided to replace the earlier churches of Hag. Eirēnē and Hag. Sophia, both of which had been destroyed in the Nikē riot. A second phase of Hag. Eirēnē dates from 564, still within Justinian's reign, when a fire, according to chronicles, destroyed the narthex and atrium. An earthquake's destruction in 740 and a subsequent reconstruction mark the third phase.

George distinguished the three building phases of Hag. Eirēnē by the three principal kinds of masonry evident in the building. The lower courses of hewn stone reaching up to the first cornice in the nave piers he attributed to Justinian's first campaign. The even courses of brick relieved by occasional bands of greenstone, a masonry style found chiefly in the narthex and atrium, he took to represent Justinian's rebuilding of these sections after the 564 fire. George then assigned all the higher portions of the church, some of them constructed of pure brick and others of alternating bands of brick and stone, to the third, eighth century phase. Included in George's hypothesis, which is supported and repeated by Van Millingen, is a reconstruction of the church in its first phase as a building somewhat shorter than the present structure, with its narthex further to the east. George identified the intermediate piers, still extant in the western bay of the church, as supports of the original narthex. Ebersolt, meanwhile, without the benefit of George's research, minimized the effects of the eighth century earthquake and assigned almost the entire fabric to the Justinianic period.

In recent times, three further archaeological studies have been done at Hag. Eirēnē. Ramazanoğlu and Dirimtekin excavated areas in the church's surroundings, uncovering on the south side a series of corridors, a courtyard, and the original stair ramp leading to the gallery, and to the northeast a round building, evidently the skeuophylakion. Dirimtekin's excavation, unfortunately, was not stratigraphically controlled and yielded less useful information than it should have. In another study, Grossman surveyed the atrium and found sufficient evidence to reconstruct the original arcading in the manner of Hagia Sophia's atrium, with piers that alternate regularly with two columns. Contrary to George's theories, Grossman's work on the atrium and Strube's more recent study of the narthex establish both atrium and narthex as integral parts of the first Justinianic phase.

Currently Urs Peschlow of the German Archaeological Institute is engaged in a more refined survey of the building and its surroundings. Peschlow's survey, which has not yet been published, has turned up evidence of a second stair ramp north of the narthex as well as evidence that the atrium was originally a two-storied structure.

The importance of the liturgical layout of Hag. Eirēnē is discussed in my previous study; much important evidence, however, doubtless remains to be uncovered in this area. Inside the church, soundings under the Turkish pavements, tentatively begun by Ramazanoğlu in 1946, are one promising direction for further study. The Turkish modifications of the vaulting, especially the main dome, are still unexplored. The heavy, helmeted appearance that now characterizes the dome cannot possibly represent its original profile.

In 1973 the Ministry of Cultural Affairs began a new excavation of the north and east sides of the church, the results of which have not yet been published.

Bibliography

Van Millingen, *Byzantine Churches*, pp. 84–105.

W.S. George, *The Church of Saint Eirene at Constantinople* (London, 1913).

Ebersolt and Thiers, *Les églises*, pp. 55–72.

M. Ramazanoğlu, "Neue Forschungen zur Architekturgeschichte der Irenenkirche und des Complexes der Sophienkirche," *Atti del VIII congresso di studi bizantini* 2, *Studi bizantini e neoellenici*, 8 (Palermo, 1951), 232–35.

F. Dirimtekin, "Les fouilles faites en 1946–47 et en 1958–60 entre Sainte-Sophie et Sainte-Irène à Istanbul," *CA* 13 (1962), 161–85.

P. Grossman, "Zum Atrium der Irenenkirche in Istanbul," *IM* 15 (1965), 186–207.

Janin, *La géographie*, pp. 103–6.

Mathews, *The Early Churches of Constantinople*, pp. 77–88.

C. Strube, *Die westliche Eingangsseite der Kirchen von Konstantinopel in justinianischer Zeit* (Weisbaden, 1973), pp. 106–17.

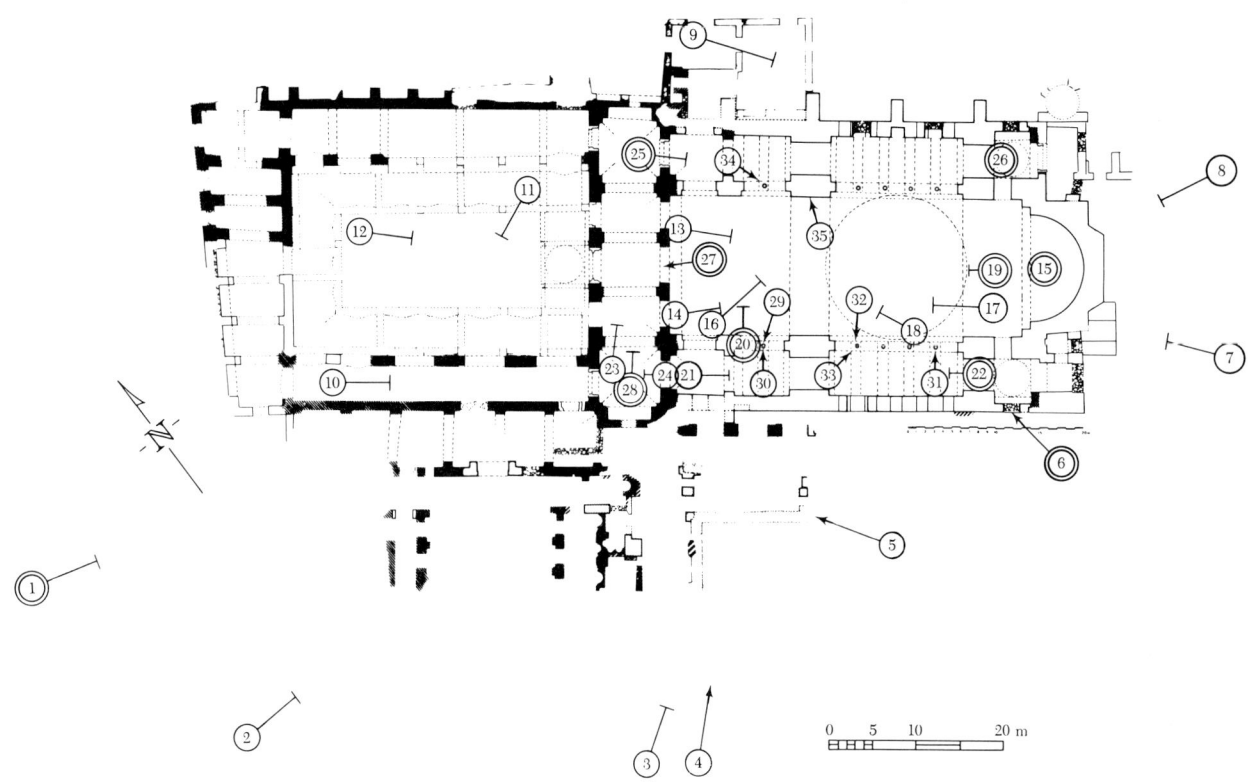

from Peschlow

104 Hag. Eirēnē

11-1

11-2

11-1 General view from the west, with the outer wall of the Topkapı Sarayı in the foreground. M4522
11-2 General view from the southwest, showing the excavation along the south side. M8926

11-3

11-3 The south flank of the church. M25709
11-4 The south flank, detail of the west bay. M12612

11-4

11-5

11-6

11-7

108 Hag. Eirēnē

11-5 The south stair ramp from the east. M6922

11-6 Capital in the southeast gallery window. M9017

11-7 The east end of the church, c. 1925. Photo Marburg, 30544

11-8

11-9

11-8 The east end of the church at present. M18404
11-9 The north flank, viewed from the northwest. Photo Urs Peschlow, the German Archaeological Institute, Istanbul.

11-10

110   Hag. Eirēnē

11-11

11-10 The south corridor of the atrium viewed from the west. M14340
11-11 The atrium from the northeast corner. M3324
11-12 The atrium and the west façade of the church. M3326

11-12

11-13

Hag. Eirēnē

11-14

11-15

11-13 General view of the nave and sanctuary from the west. M7016
11-14 General view of the nave and south gallery from the west. M20602
11-15 Apse vaulting with iconoclastic mosaic. M20558

11-16

114   Hag. Eirēnē

11-17

11-18

11-16 The north wall and the north piers supporting the dome, from the southwest. M20614
11-17 General view of the nave from the sanctuary in 1974. M60133A
11-18 Western bay of the nave, viewed from the southeast. M20620

11-19

11-20

11-19 Vaulting of the nave with the main dome above, in 1974. M60128
11-20 Sail-vault over the western bay of the nave, viewed from the south. M20644
11-21 South aisle, viewed from the west. M14366

11-21

11-22

11-23

11-24

11-22 Vaulting in the south aisle, viewed from the east. M20762
11-23 The narthex, viewed from the south. M14316
11-24 Entrance from the south corridor of the atrium to the narthex. M6929
11-25 The north gallery, viewed from the west. M20704

11-25

Hag. Eirēnē

11-26

11-27

11-28

Hag. Eirēnē

11-29

11-26 Vaulting of the northeast chamber in the gallery. M7027
11-27 Parapets in the narthex gallery, viewed from the nave. M7012
11-28 The narthex gallery, viewed from the south. M3509
11-29 Fifth capital in the south aisle colonnade, viewed from the nave. M6936

11-30

11-31

11-32

11-33

11-34

11-35

11-30 Fifth capital in the south aisle colonnade, viewed from the aisle. M20744
11-31 First capital in the south aisle colonnade, viewed from the aisle. M20754
11-32 Fourth capital in the south aisle colonnade, viewed from the nave. M7001
11-33 Fourth capital in the south aisle colonnade, viewed from the aisle. M20736
11-34 Fifth capital in the north aisle colonnade, viewed from the aisle. M14426
11-35 Detail of the base molding on the great center pier on the north side of the nave. M20770

12

Hag. Euphēmia en tō Hippodromō (St. Euphemia at the Hippodrome)

The discovery in 1939, near the Hippodrome, of frescoes representing the life and martyrdom of St. Euphemia led to the ready identification of the ruins of that saint's church. The subsequent excavation, carried out by the German Archaeological Institute under Schneider's direction, uncovered the remains of a powerfully built hexagonal structure which originally belonged to the fifth century palace of Antiochus, a praepositus under Theodosius II.

The loss of Schneider's excavation diaries rendered the final report by Naumann and Belting less definitive than it should have been, but the principal archaeological facts are fairly well established. The height of the standing walls varies between 1 and 3 meters, and they clearly show that the building, which was entered from a sigma-plan colonnade, featured a large niche on each of the six sides, and exterior porches between the niches that served as auxiliary entrances. At some time in the sixth century, apparently, the secular palace structure was converted into a church; this involved reorienting the building slightly by opening up a new entrance in the west niche and inserting a sanctuary in the east. The remains of the synthronon, altar foundation, chancel barrier, and solea found on the site, all conforming to sixth century style characteristics, have served as evidence in dating the church's founding, and were important for the reconstruction of Early Byzantine ceremonial.

Grabar tried to interpret the church as primarily a martyrium, locating the remains of St. Euphemia outside the sanctuary in the northeast niche; but archaeology does not seem to support this. Furthermore, literary sources tell us that when the saint's remains were transported here from Chalcedon in the seventh century, they were then placed in a small box under the altar.

The church continued in use down to the Turkish Conquest. It was visited by medieval pilgrims, as Janin narrates, and was redecorated in Palaeologan times with frescoes, some of which survive in the southwest part of the church, where they are now housed in a protective shed.

Bibliography

K. Bittel and A.M. Schneider, "Das Martyrion der hl. Euphemia beim Hippodrom," *AA* 56 (1941), 296–315.

R. Naumann and H. Belting, *Die Euphemia-Kirche am Hippodrom zu Istanbul und ihre Fresken*, Istanbuler Forschungen, 25 (Berlin, 1966).

A. Grabar, "Études critiques: R. Naumann, Die Euphemiakirche," *CA* 17 (1967), 251–54.

Janin, *La géographie*, pp. 120–24.

Mathews, *The Early Churches of Constantinople*, pp. 61–67.

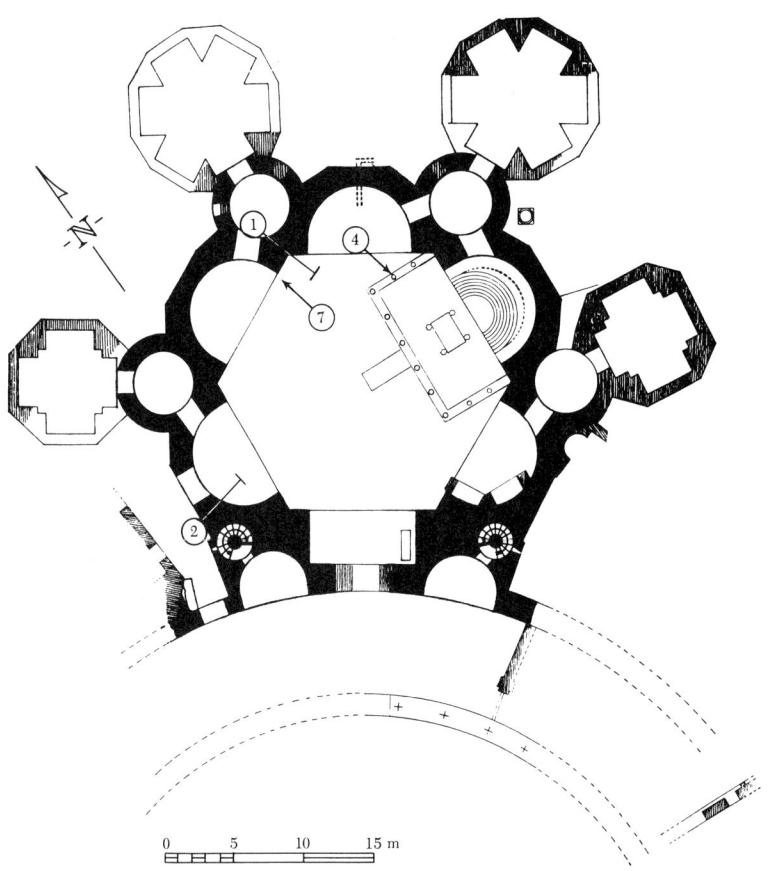

from Naumann

12-1 The sanctuary, viewed from the northwest, in 1942. Photo Artamonoff, courtesy Dumbarton Oaks Field Committee

12-2

12-3

12-2 General view from the west. M6618
12-3 Inlaid colonnette from the sanctuary enclosure, now in the Istanbul Archaeological Museum. Photo courtesy the German Archaeological Institute, 2237
12-4 Sanctuary stylobate (reused). M5526
12-5 Column base from the sanctuary enclosure. M5505
12-6 Capital from the sanctuary enclosure. M5504
12-7 Masonry detail of the north pier. M5521

12-4

12-5

12-6

12-7

Hag. Euphēmia en tō Hippodromō

13

Gül Camii

Scholarship concerning this imposing monument of Byzantine architecture has revolved around two principal problems—the problem of distinguishing the original Byzantine elements from the Turkish parts, and that of identifying the church in Byzantine historical sources. Neither problem has yet been resolved, but Schäfer's recent dissertation on the Gül Camii has helped to eliminate some unnecessary speculation on both issues.

Regarding the identification of the church, earlier scholars had selected Hag. Theodosia en tois Dexiokratous as most likely; but they were embarrassed by the fact that mention of such a church is not found until at least the fourteenth century, whereas the building in question seemed to be considerably older. To resolve this difficulty, Pargoire worked out an ingenious hypothesis, later accepted by Janin: the building, he supposed, was originally Hag. Euphēmia en tō Petriō, a ninth century foundation of Basil I which was known to have contained the relics of St. Theodosia. According to the theory, the church assumed a dedication to the second saint, but only gradually, and this explains the absence of earlier references to this identification.

The problem with Pargoire's hypothesis, as Schäfer has now shown, is the ninth century date, which archaeologists had believed secure because of the church's cross-domed plan. According to Schäfer, the Gül Camii, like several other churches in Istanbul, rests on a great vaulted podium or platform, the masonry of which is uniform with that of the original sections of the upper church—courses of recessed brick and courses of stone, with occasional vertical bricks. This kind of work is known not to precede the end of the tenth century in Constantinople; the founding of the church must be dated roughly 1000–1150.

However, beyond establishing the general limits of dating, Schäfer's monograph is far from definitive, and his suggested identification of the Gül Camii as Christos Euergetēs is not confirmed by the sources.

Between the Turkish Conquest and the founding of the mosque of the Gül, more than a century intervened, during which the building apparently suffered considerable damage. At present the interior is still heavily plastered, and differences between Byzantine and Turkish construction can only be surmised from inconsistencies in cornice lines, pilasters, and vault springings. Van Millingen, Ebersolt, and Brunov, all of whom misdated the original building as ninth century, correctly noted that the low dome, and its support on four pointed arches springing from pilasters, were Turkish. The east end of the church, with its barrel-vaulted sanctuary and its flanking chapels on ground and gallery level (with two miniature chapels between the two levels), is clearly Byzantine. The rebuilding of the central apse also appears to be Byzantine work, but its irregularities are difficult to explain. Of the north, west, and south barrel vaults, it is not known how much is still original fabric. If, as Schäfer believes, the entire southwest corner has been rebuilt, then the south and west vaults are Turkish reconstructions. Schäfer points out that the galleries are now about half a meter higher than they were originally. Another Turkish alteration has replaced the original narthex with a wooden porch.

Bibliography

J. Pargoire, "Constantinople: L'église Sainte-Théodosie," *EO* 9 (1906), 161–65.

Van Millingen, *Byzantine Churches,* pp. 164–82.

Ebersolt and Thiers, *Les églises,* pp. 113–27.

N. Brunov, "Die Gül-Djami von Konstantinopel," *BZ* 30 (1929–30), 554–60.

Janin, *La géographie,* pp. 127–29, 143–45.

H. Schäfer, *Die Gül Camii in Istanbul: Ein Beitrag zur mittelbyzantinischen Kirchenarchitektur Konstantinopels,* IM Beiheft 7 (Tübingen, 1973).

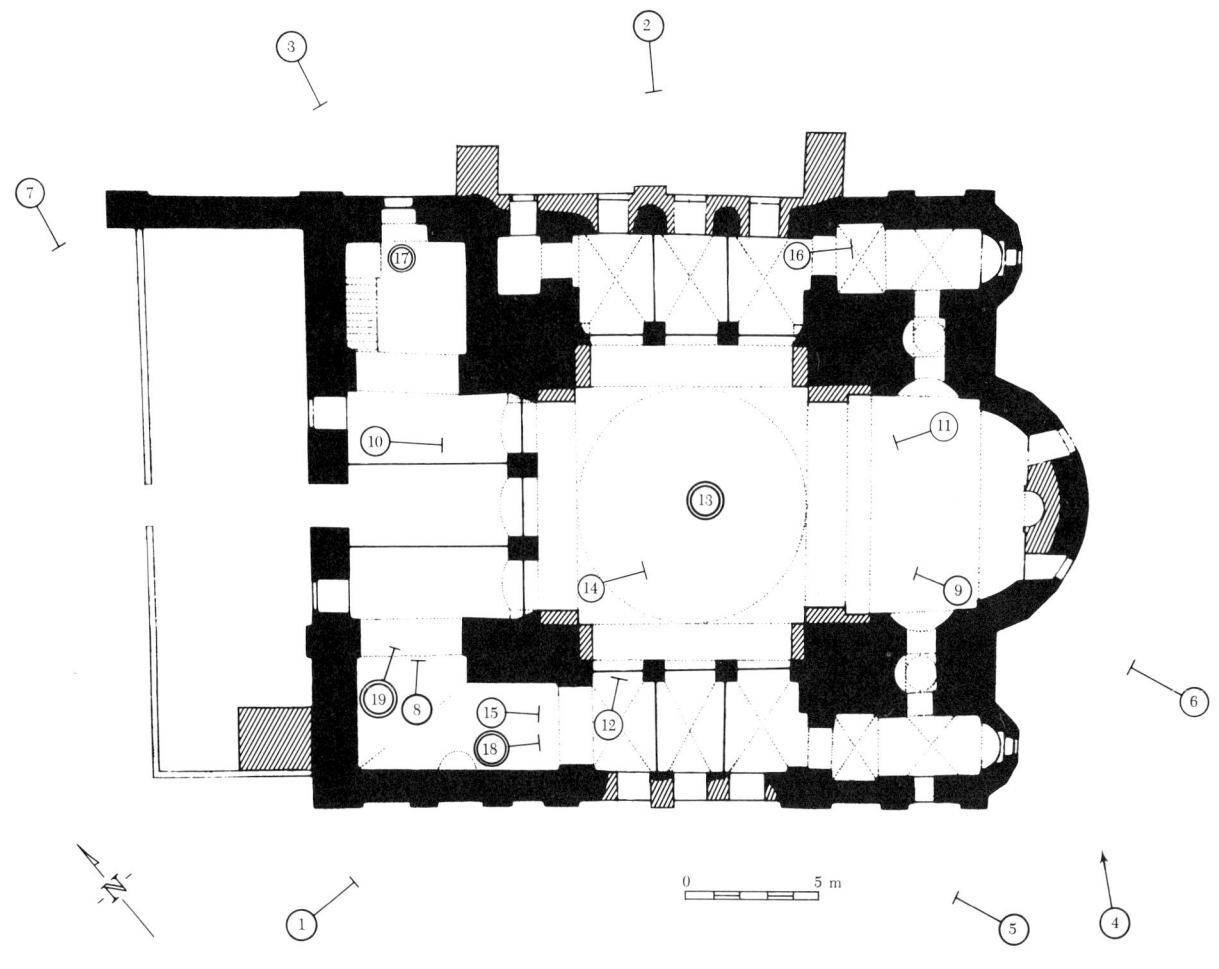

from Ebersolt

13-1

13-2

13-3

13-1   General view from the southwest. M22052
13-2   The north flank of the church. M26220
13-3   General view from the northwest. M19517

Gül Camii   131

13-5

13-6

13-4   Detail of the east end, viewed from the southeast. M15650
13-5   South flank, viewed from the southeast. M15658
13-6   The east end of the church. M22916

13-7

13-8

13-9

134   Gül Camii

13-10

13-7 The west façade during the reconstruction of the Turkish porch, c. 1940.
Eski Eserleri Koruma Encümeni, 3662, Istanbul Archaeological Museum
13-8 The west ambulatory viewed from the south. M23918
13-9 View of the nave from the sanctuary, with the west ambulatory on the left. M24003A
13-10 View from the west ambulatory into the nave. M24001

13-11

13-12

13-13

13-14

13-11 General view from the sanctuary, with the southwest pier on the left. M24007A
13-12 The north crossarm viewed from the south ambulatory. M24014
13-13 The dome, with the east barrel vault at right. M7254
13-14 The sanctuary. M23914

13-15

13-16

13-15 The south ambulatory, viewed from the west. M7236
13-16 The prothesis chapel. M7218
13-17 The vaulting of the northwest corner bay, with the north wall below. M7313
13-18 The south gallery from the west. M7274
13-19 The west gallery from the southwest. M7270

13-17

13-18

13-19

Gül Camii 139

14

Hag. Iōannēs Prodromos en tō Hebdomō
(St. John the Forerunner in Hebdomon)

Erected by Justinian shortly before 555, this monument supplies us with an important parallel to S. Vitale in Ravenna. Janin has traced the history of the church, its connection with the palace at Hebdomon (modern Bakırköy) and the role it played in coronation ceremonial, and its apparent decline and ruin in the Middle Byzantine period, when the palace itself declined in importance. What little remained of the church in the twentieth century, a few pier foundations and part of the apse, was excavated by the French Army in 1921–23; but the excavation was not very exacting in its archaeological standards, and the report on it, published by Demangel in 1945, was not very careful in its reading of literary sources. The site now no longer exists, having been cleared in 1965 for the construction of a hospital.

My own study in 1971 proposed a reconstruction of the monument on the basis of literary sources matched with the archaeological information. According to this reconstruction, the Hebdomon church, like S. Vitale, consisted basically of a domed octagonal core surrounded by an octagonal ambulatory and gallery zone; its inner core, like those of both S. Vitale and Hag. Sergios and Bacchus, expanded into the surrounding zone with a series of large niches. This design firmly places the structure in the important new group of central-planned churches, introduced by Justinian, that was so decisive to the course of Byzantine architecture. Even the dimensions of the Hebdomon church are surprisingly close to those of S. Vitale, except that here the dome was wider, requiring a heavier series of buttressing piers in the ambulatory. The apse, semicircular inside and out, lay above a small crypt, which could be entered from both north and south sides outside the apse. Literary sources tell us also that the church had a porch and surrounding courtyard, and that the building was richly finished in marble and gold.

Bibliography

R. Demangel, *Contribution à la topographie de l'Hebdomon* (Paris, 1945), pp. 17–32.

Janin, *La géographie*, pp. 413–15.

Mathews, *The Early Churches of Constantinople*, pp. 55–61.

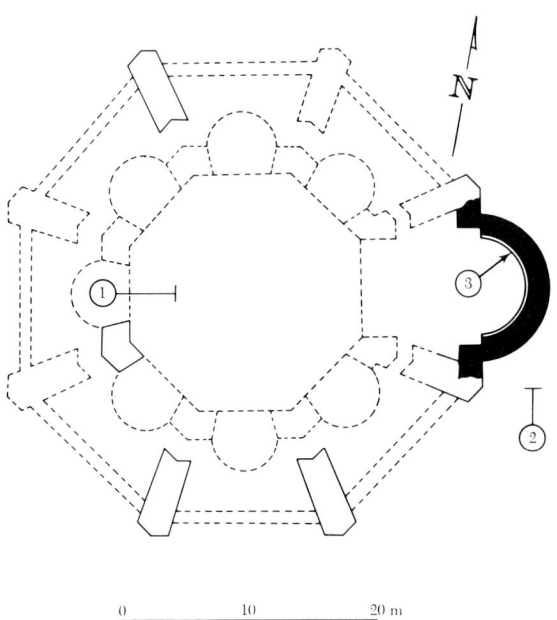

from Mathews

14-1 The apse from the west, during demolition in 1965. Photo W. Kleiss, German Archaeological Institute, Istanbul, R6

14-2

14-4

14-3

14-5

14-2 The exterior of the apse from the south, 1949. Photo C. Mango, Dumbarton Oaks Field Committee, L.49.163
14-3 Detail of the masonry inside the apse, 1949. Photo C. Mango, Dumbarton Oaks Field Committee, L.49.161
14-4 Ionic impost capital, now in the garden of Hagia Sophia. M4910
14-5 Inlaid column, now in the Istanbul Archaeological Museum, no. 3908. M1714

15

Hag. Iōannēs Prodromos en tois Stoudiou (St. John the Forerunner in the Stoudios Estates). Mirahor (Imrahor) Mescidi. Ilyas Bey Mescidi.

The spacious and well-proportioned basilica which Senator Stoudios founded near the Golden Gate is the oldest church in Constantinople of which substantial portions still stand, and it is therefore a key monument in the history of Byzantine architecture. At the same time, it is of great significance to Byzantine religious history. This was the most important shrine of the Baptist within the walls of the city, and the monastery associated with the church played a major role in resolving the iconoclastic dispute and in setting the style for eastern monastic life in general, from Russia to the Balkans. Conflicting sources date the church either in 463 or shortly before 454.

Despite the monument's obvious importance, no adequate excavation of the site or survey of the building has ever been completed. The only serious attempt was that made by the Russian Archaeological Institute under Panchenko in 1907–9. This excavation succeeded in clearing the site of the debris of the Mirahor Mescidi, a structure which had fallen to ruin in 1894, and went on to uncover the lovely inlaid marble pavement as well as the cruciform crypt under the altar. But the undertaking was broken off over political difficulties and never resumed. A series of fifth century reliefs removed by the Russians from burial sites in the south aisle are now in the Istanbul Archaeological Museum and were described in Mendel's catalogue.

The most thorough and accurate plan of the church is that provided by Ebersolt, although it should be supplemented by Van Millingen's plans and sections, and by the plan and section of the crypt published later by Bittel, as well as by my survey and reconstruction of the atrium and the sanctuary.

The design that emerges from the research to date is an eminently logical and straightforward one. The nave and aisles of the church form an almost perfectly square unit, which is preceded by an atrium, including the narthex, of roughly the same square dimensions. The extraordinary openness of the interior space is enhanced by the large number of entrances giving access to the building from all four sides, and by galleries running above the aisles and above the narthex; the galleries were originally reached by stairways from the outside. Both Deichmann and Krautheimer have remarked on the almost cubical proportions of the church's interior spaces, proportions which may testify to the continuation of a classic basilica style from as far back as Constantinian times.

The decoration of the building, much of it still in evidence, was very rich in color and detail, with handsome door and window frames, columns and chancel fittings in green marble, crisply carved capitals and entablatures, and bright marble revetment everywhere. The architectural sculpture has been discussed by Kautzsch and Deichmann; but as an essential link in the century of development from the Theodosian style to the mature Justinianic style, it deserves closer scrutiny. Notice has been made, meanwhile, by Ettinghausen of a find of Middle Byzantine wall tiles from the site, perhaps contemporary with the inlaid pavement.

Of the monastery once attached to the church, only a cistern remains, located to the southeast of the building. According to Gourlay, a two-columned, groin-vaulted chapel of Middle or Late Byzantine construction formerly existed over a corner of the cistern, and this is documented in photographs by Artamonoff.

Since the Russian excavation the site of the Stoudios has undergone alternating periods of neglect and fits of restoration, during which much evidence has been lost. Most of the charming animals in the inlaid floor have disappeared, and a great deal of the masonry has been repointed. Older photographs are therefore indispensable. The photographs of Esat Tengizman, in the Eski Eserleri Koruma Encümeni, especially deserve to be better known.

Bibliography

C. Gourlay, "Minor Churches of Constantinople," *JRIBA* 14, 18 (1907), 637–49.

B. Panchenko, "Ha. Iōannēs Studios," *Izvestiya russkago arkeol. instituta* 14 (Sofia, 1909), 136–52; 15 (1911), 250–57; 16 (1912), 1–359.

Ebersolt and Thiers, *Les églises*, pp. 3–18.

Van Millingen, *Byzantine Churches*, pp. 35–61.

G. Mandel, *Catalogue des sculptures grecques, romaines et byzantines* (Istanbul, 1912–14), nos. 668–70, 715–22, 1209.

R. Kautzsch, *Kapitellstudien. Studien zur spätentiken Kunstgeschichte* 9 (Berlin-Leipzig, 1936), pp. 131, 135–36, 167.

K. Bittel, *AA* 64 (1939), 202, fig. 51–52.

E. Ettinghausen, "Byzantine Tiles from the Basilica in the Topkapu Sarayi and Saint John of Stoudios," *CA* 7 (1954), 79–88.

F.W. Deichmann, *Studien zur Architektur Konstantinopels*, Deutsche Beiträge zur Altertumswissenschaft (Baden-Baden, 1956), pp. 56–108.

Krautheimer, *Early Christian and Byzantine Architecture*, pp. 78–79.

Janin, *La géographie*, pp. 430–40.

Mathews, *The Early Churches of Constantinople*, pp. 19–27.

15-1 General view from the northwest, c. 1925. Photo Esat Tengizman, courtesy Eski Eserleri Koruma Encümeni, 634, Istanbul Archaeological Museum

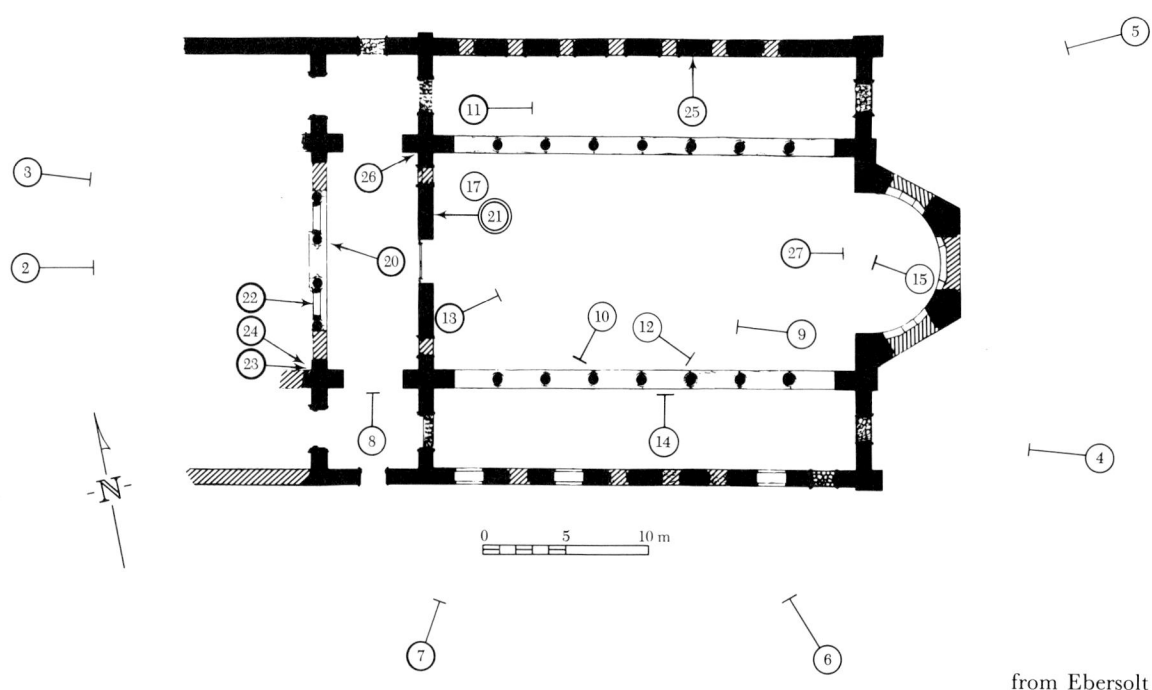

from Ebersolt

15-2

146 Hag. Iōannēs Prodromos en tois Stoudiou

15-3

15-2 The narthex façade at present. M9332
15-3 The narthex façade, c. 1925. Photo Esat Tengizman, courtesy Eski Eserleri Koruma Encümeni, 626, Istanbul Archaeological Museum

15-4

15-4 Detail of the east end, showing the east entrance to the south aisle, c. 1925. Photo Esat Tengizman, courtesy Eski Eserleri Koruma Encümeni, 638, Istanbul Archaeological Museum
15-5 The east end. M5305
15-6 The south flank of the church, c. 1925. Photo Esat Tengizman, courtesy Eski Eserleri Koruma Encümeni, 636, Istanbul Archaeological Museum
15-7 The south flank at present. M25415

15-5

15-6

15-7

15-8

15-9

150 Hag. Iōannēs Prodromos en tois Stoudiou

15-10

15-8 The narthex, viewed from the south. M9426
15-9 General interior view from the east, c. 1925. Photo Esat Tengizman, courtesy Eski Eserleri Koruma Encümeni, 649, Istanbul Archaeological Museum
15-10 Interior view of the southwest corner, c. 1925. Photo Esat Tengizman, Eski Eserleri Koruma Encümeni, 653, Istanbul Archaeological Museum

15-11

152   Hag. Iōannēs Prodromos en tois Stoudiou

15-12

15-13

15-11 The north aisle, from the west. M3306
15-12 Interior view of the southeast corner, c. 1920. Photo A.K. Porter Collection, 5342, the Fogg Art Museum, Harvard University
15-13 View toward the sanctuary. M3303

15-14

15-15

154 Hag. Iōannēs Prodromos en tois Stoudiou

15-16

15-17

15-18

15-19

15-14 The north wall and the north aisle colonnade, from the south. M14663
15-15 General view of the pavement from the east. M14864
15-16 Pavement detail, a griffon, c. 1920. Photo Sender, rephotographed. M22513
15-17 Pavement detail, a flying griffon. M3236
15-18 Pavement detail, a fox, since destroyed, c. 1920. Photo Sender, rephotographed. M22512
15-19 Pavement detail, a rabbit, since destroyed, c. 1920. Photo Sender, rephotographed. M22509

15-20

15-21

15-22

15-23

15-24

15-20 Narthex capital, the second from the north. M14750
15-21 Fragment of the entablature from the west wall of the nave, during restoration, 1943. Eski Eserleri Koruma Encümeni, 654, Istanbul Archaeological Museum
15-22 A detail of dentils on the cornice of the narthex façade. Photo German Archaeological Institute, Istanbul, Kb. 1428
15-23 Detail of Fig. 15-24. Photo German Archaeological Institute, Istanbul, Kb. 1428
15-24 The entablature and the pilaster capital at the south end of the narthex façade. M317

15-25

15-26

15-27

15-28

15-29

15-25 Detail of the masonry and a window in the north aisle. M14833
15-26 Detail of the base molding in the narthex. M14819
15-27 Crypt entrance and remains of the synthronon in the apse, intersected by Turkish Mihrab wall, 1955. Photo R. Hamann-MacLean, Bildarchiv Foto Marburg, 229160
15-28 Chapel southeast of the church, c. 1940. Photo Artamonoff, Dumbarton Oaks Field Committee, RA479b
15-29 The interior of the chapel southeast of the church, c. 1940. Photo Artamonoff, Dumbarton Oaks Field Committee, RA476a

16

Hag. Iōannēs Prodromos en tō Troullō (St. John the Forerunner at the Dome).   Ahmet Paşa Camii. Hırami Ahmet Paşa Camii.

The dedication of this diminutive church is firmly established by records of its continued Christian use well into the sixteenth century, but otherwise little is known of its history. A few pages by Van Millingen constitute the only archaeological report on the monument, and the entire fabric of the building was restored with a heavy hand. A valuable set of photographs in the Dumbarton Oaks archive bears witness to the losses and changes that occurred.

The structure had languished in ruins for several decades before the Ministry of Mosques undertook its restoration in 1960. At this time the vaulting of the narthex, most of which had fallen, was rebuilt, and the walled-up windows were reopened. The mullions and capitals of the north nave window were reinstated, and four handsome antique columns and capitals were introduced to replace those removed when the structure had been converted to a mosque. Unhappily, the restorers made no systematic study of the church and they destroyed much valuable evidence. The frescoes remarked upon by earlier visitors perished during the cleaning; and the masonry was refinished throughout, even to the point of resurfacing much of the exterior with freshly hewn stone blocks.

Although scholars seem generally to agree on a twelfth century date for the Troullō church, there is room for conjecture. The unusual east end of the church, with its three semicircular apses, seems to support this dating, when it is compared to the plan of the Sekbanbaşı. On the other hand, the outlining of the extrados of the window arches in the cupola parallels that in the cupola of the Panagiotissa, a church usually identified as a Palaeologan foundation.

Bibliography

Van Millingen, *Byzantine Churches*, pp. 201–6.
Janin, *La géographie*, pp. 441–42.

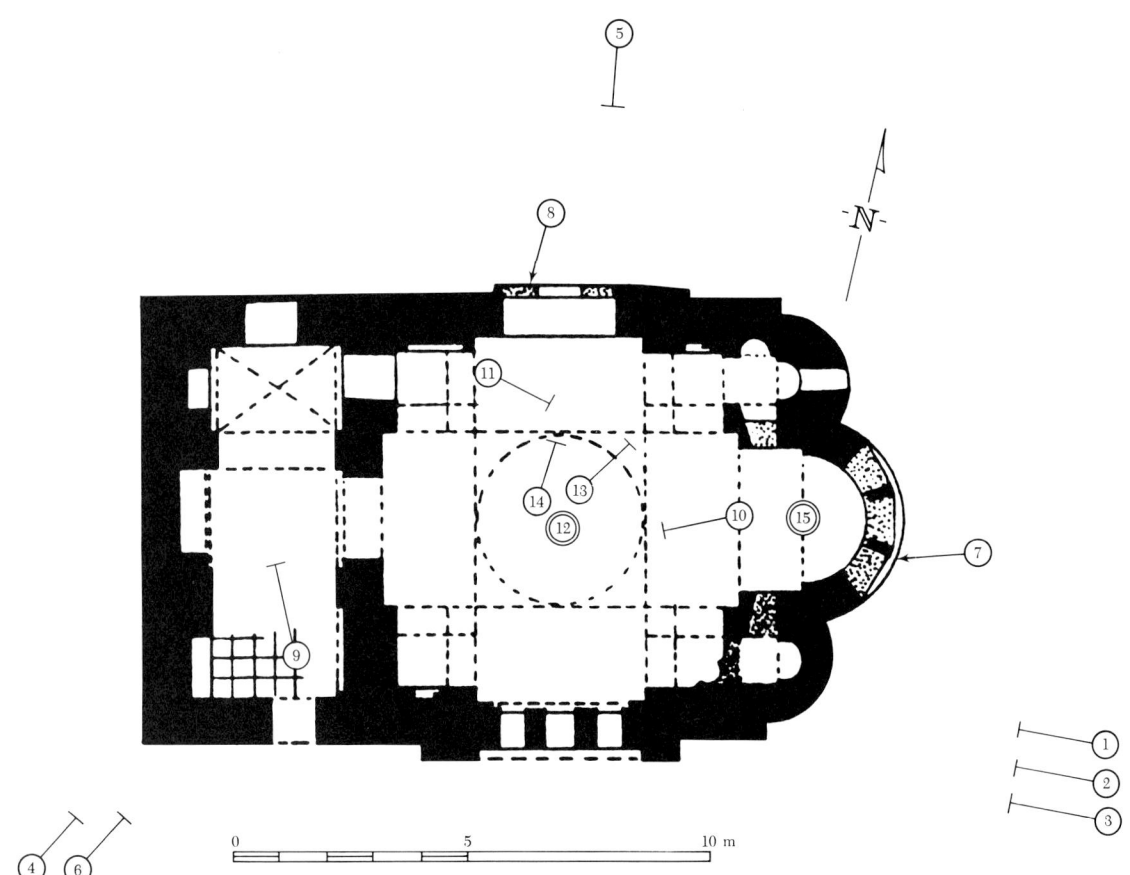

from Van Millingen

16-1

16-2

Hag. Iōannēs Prodromos en tō Troullō

16-3

16-1   The east end of the church during restoration, 1960. Photo Dumbarton Oaks Field Committee, H.60.144
16-2   The east end in its present state. M15354
16-3   The east end of the church, c. 1935. Photo Artamonoff, Dumbarton Oaks Field Committee, RA186b

16-4

16-4 View from the southwest, in its present state. M23207
16-5 The north flank of the church. M15350
16-6 View from the southwest, c. 1935. Photo Artamonoff, Dumbarton Oaks Field Committee, RA186a RA186a
16-7 Capital in the apse window. M15340
16-8 Capital in the north window. M10913

16-5

16-6

16-7

16-8

16-9

16-9 The narthex, viewed from the south. M7714
16-10 General view of the interior from the east. M15366
16-11 View of the sanctuary and prothesis chapel. M3835

16-10

Hag. Iōannēs Prodromos en tō Troullō

16-11

16-12

166 Hag. Iōannēs Prodromos en tō Troullō

16-13

16-15

16-12 The dome and pendentives, with the east below. M7726
16-13 The northwest corner of the interior, 1957. Photo Dumbarton Oaks Field Committee, H.57.414
16-14 Detail of the north wall. M3837
16-15 The vaulting of the apse. M7677

17

Isa Kapısı Mescidi. Manastir Mescidi. Ibrahim Paşa Mescidi.

The best study of this church to date is still the summary treatment offered by its "discoverers" Alpatov and Brunov in 1925. Schneider, ten years later, attempted to carry the research further, but his brief report garbles the dimensions of the building and also presents a plan that fails to distinguish between what the author observed and what he was reconstructing. The plan further complicates matters by the inclusion of an unlikely seven-windowed apse which contradicts the evidence on the site. The only additional archaeological account of the monument is that done by Eyice, who merely recapitulates earlier information. In the meantime, a heavy growth of bramble and vine has claimed most of the structure, and will have to be removed before any new investigation is possible.

The design of the Isa is unusual in Byzantine architecture, and certainly merits more study. The building clearly had a long nave, timber-roofed and apparently undivided, ending in a triple barrel-vaulted sanctuary at the east end. When the church was converted to the mosque of Ibrahim Paşa, its central apse was reduced to a flat exterior and a minaret was inserted in place of its prothesis. Then, in 1894, an earthquake brought down the roof and most of the north and west walls. The Isa has been a ruin since that time, and even the few fresco remnants observable a few years ago in the diaconicon chapel have all but disappeared.

Alpatov and Brunov observed a significant similarity between the decorative brick motifs on the building's south exterior and the decoration of the Pammakaristos and the Kariye Camii parekklesions. These closely worked checkerboards, zigzags, and banded voussoirs, now hidden by undergrowth, effectively assure that the Isa is a Palaeologan structure. As to the church's dedication, meanwhile, nothing is yet known, as Janin indicates.

Bibliography

M. Alpatov and N. Brunov, "Une nouvelle église de l'époque des Paléologues à Constantinople," *EO* 24 (1925), 14–25.

Schneider, *Byzanz*, pp. 5–7.

R. Janin, "La topographie de Constantinople byzantine: études et découvertes, 1918 38," *EO* 38 (1939), 144–45.

Eyice, *Son devir Bizans Mimarisi*, pp. 29–31.

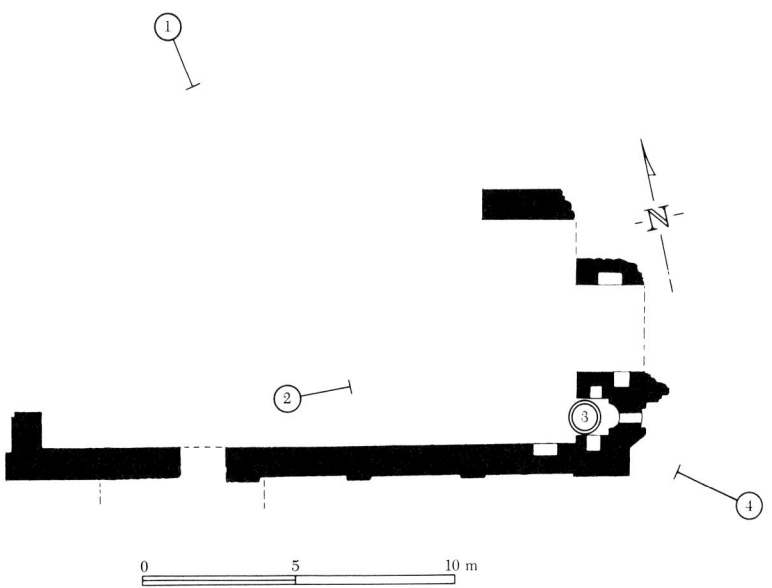

from Alpatov

17-1 General view of the site from the northwest, 1935. Photo Eski Eserleri Koruma Encümeni, 1463, Istanbul Archaeological Museum

17-2

17-3

17-4

17-2 View of the sanctuary and diaconicon chapel from the west, 1935. Photo Eski Eserleri Koruma Encümeni, 1467, Istanbul Archaeological Museum
17-3 Vaulting of the diaconicon chapel. M13723
17-4 Exterior detail of the diaconicon chapel. M21412

18

Kalenderhane Camii

The excavation by Striker and Kuban, still in progress at the Kalenderhane Camii, has so thoroughly revised our picture of this monument as to render earlier work largely obsolete. Traditionally archaeologists, starting with Freshfield, had discussed the simple, domed Greek cross of the Kalenderhane as a transitional design. Kollwitz, viewing Byzantine architecture in evolutionary terms, described the Kalenderhane as one step in the transformation from the Early Byzantine domed-basilica design to the formulation of the Middle Byzantine quincunx, or cross-in-square plan. The terms of this discussion gave wide latitude to speculation on the date of the monument, a problem that was further complicated by the reuse of Early Byzantine sculptural material in the building. However, Kollwitz proposed a ninth century date on the basis of masonry visible at that time (1934), and this dating was commonly accepted.

The Striker and Kuban excavation has put an end to this speculation. Controlled pottery finds demonstrated that the main fabric of the Greek-cross plan, that is, its barrel-vaulted arms and broad dome, cannot be dated earlier than the end of the twelfth century.

The present excavation has also clarified the plan of the building and has distinguished elements on the site that are earlier and later than the main twelfth century building phase. Foundations were discovered for outer aisles to the north and south which communicated with the crossarms through tall triple arcades on the ground level. To the west the nave opened through arcades into a narthex as well as into a narthex gallery whose remains were discovered above. The plan of the narthex and narthex gallery followed a design known at the south church of the Pantokratōr, with both stories open in the center under a single dome. The outer narthex was evidently added later. At least three earlier building phases were found at the east end of the church, and this accounts for the extraordinary irregularity of this part of the plan. Earliest were the remains of an apsed hall-church that lay up against the Aqueduct of Valens and ran obliquely under the site of the north outer aisle of the twelfth century church. This was clearly sixth century in its masonry. To the south of this was built a much larger church, possibly in the seventh century, whose barrel-vaulted sanctuary and apse were reused in the twelfth century building (the apse was destroyed in Turkish times). Further to the south are a pair of chapels of tenth or eleventh century date which were also incorporated into the later building.

The decoration of the Kalenderhane Camii was rich and elegant, and earlier archaeologists often remarked on the colorful marble revetments of the nave and elaborate icon frames flanking the sanctuary. The current excavation has also uncovered mosaic and fresco decoration, including two finds of primary importance in the history of Byzantine art. The first was a mosaic panel, one meter square, belonging to one of the pre-iconoclast phases of the site. The panel shows the Presentation in the Temple and is the earliest Byzantine mosaic of a religious subject in Constantinople. The other important find belonged to the decoration of one of the chapels at the southeast corner of the church and consisted of a series of frescoes of the life of St. Francis Assisi. These are the first paintings belonging to the Latin rule discovered in Constantinople and the earliest extant fresco cycle of the life of St. Francis.

Striker's redating of the Kalenderhane Camii to the twelfth century has left in doubt the earlier efforts to identify the church either as Theotokos tōn Diakonissēs or as Christos ho Akataleptos. In neither instance did the sources refer to a twelfth century church, and in both cases the topographical information was rather vague. To further complicate the question, a donor fresco in the southeast chapel and another fresco over the main entrance to the narthex were both found to carry the figure of the Mother-of-God with the inscription "Kyriotissa." The prominence given to this rather uncommon theme suggests that such might in fact have been the dedication of the church.

Bibliography

E. Freshfield, "Notes on the Church Now Called the Mosque of the Kalenders at Constantinople," *Archaeologia* 55 (1897), 431–38.

Van Millingen, *Byzantine Churches*, pp. 183–90.

Ebersolt and Thiers, *Les églises*, pp. 93–110.

N. Brunov, "Zur Erforschung der Byzantinischen Baudenkmäler von Konstantinopel," *BZ* 32 (1932), 49–62.

J. Kollwitz, "Zur frühmittelalterlichen Baukunst Konstantinopels," *Römische Quartalschrift* 42 (1934), 233–50.

Janin, *La géographie*, pp. 504–6.

C.L. Striker and Y. Doğan Kuban, "Work at Kalenderhane Camii in Istanbul," *DOP* 21 (1967), 267–71; 22 (1968), 185–93; 25 (1971), 251–58.

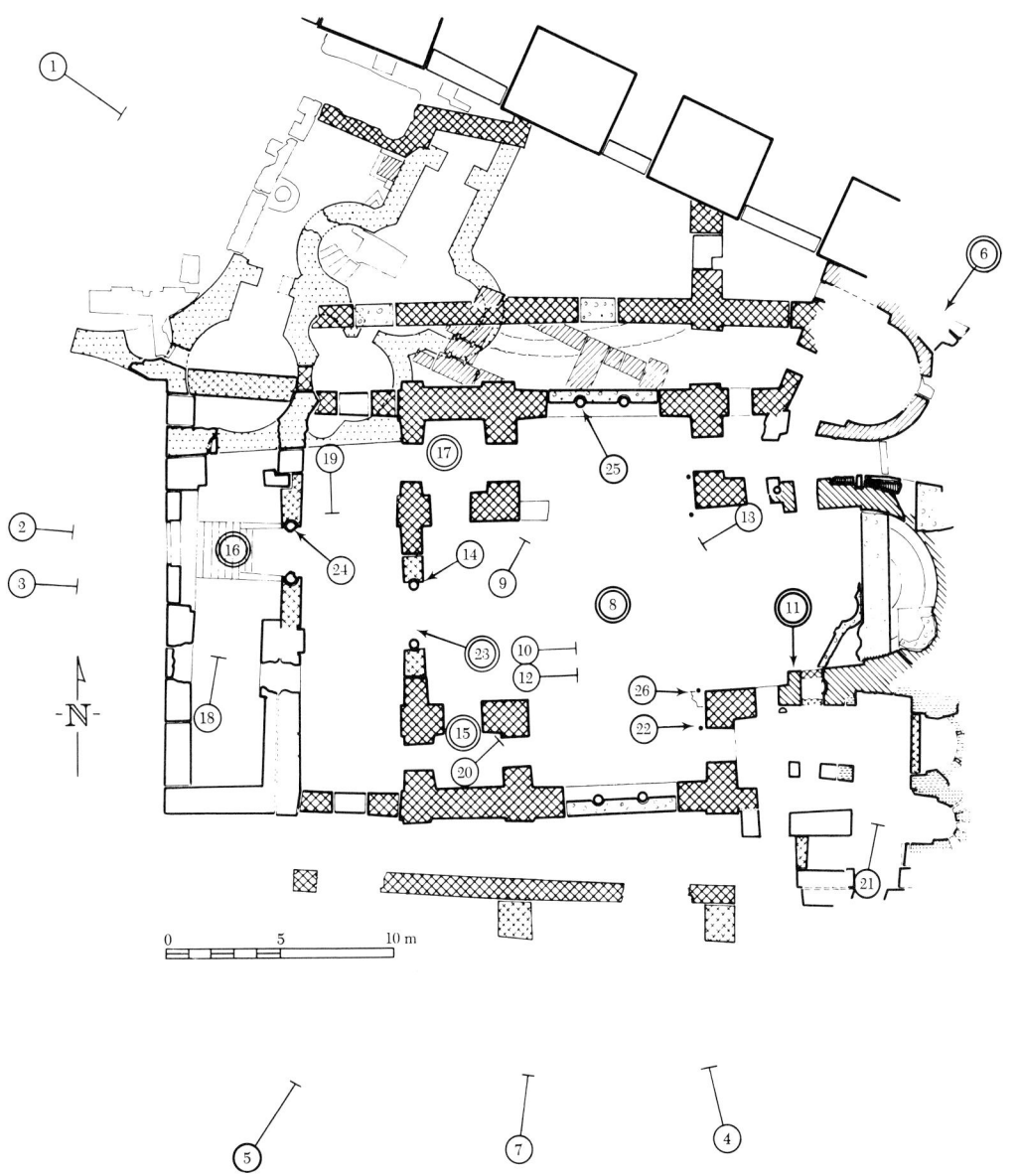

from Striker

Kalenderhane Camii

18-1

18-2

18-3

18-1 View from the northwest. M23318
18-2 The west façade. M26530
18-3 The west façade c. 1940, before the restoration. Eski Eserleri Koruma Encümeni, 2689, Istanbul Archaeological Museum

Kalenderhane Camii 175

18-4

18-5

176   Kalenderhane Camii

18-4 The south flank of the church. M26519
18-5 View from the southwest. M26510
18-6 The dome and detail of the northeast corner. M23813
18-7 View from the south in 1950, before the restoration. Photo Josephine Powell, T 11-1

18-6

18-7

18-8

18-8 The vaulting of the dome and crossarms, with the west below. M23530
18-9 The north arm of the church. M23607

18-9

18-10

18-11

18-10 View toward the sanctuary before the restoration. Photo R. Hamann-MacLean, Bildarchiv Foto Marburg, 229138
18-11 Detail of the south wall of the sanctuary. M23460
18-12 The sanctuary during the restoration. M23570
18-13 The southwest pier; the west crossarm at the right. M23454
18-14 Revetment on the west wall over the main entrance. Photo R. Hamann-MacLean, Bildarchiv Foto Marburg, LA1316/44

18-12

18-13

18-14

18-15

18-16

18-17

18-18

18-19

18-15   The vaulting in the southwest corner bay, with the east below. M23701
18-16   The vaulting of the outer narthex, with the north below. M23716
18-17   The vaulting (reconstructed) in the northwest gallery bay, with the east below. M23625
18-18   The outer narthex from the south, during the excavation. M23712
18-19   The inner narthex from the north. M23720

18-20

18-21

18-22

18-23

18-24

18-25

18-26

18-20 View from the southwest corner bay toward the sanctuary. M23703
18-21 The southeast chapel complex with the "Melismos" apse at the right foreground and the "St. Francis" apse beyond the ladder. M23805
18-22 Detail of lintel and capital under the icon frame south of the sanctuary. M23428
18-23 A window capital in the west wall. M23670
18-24 North capital in the door frame between the outer and inner narthex. M23808
18-25 West capital of the arcade in the north crossarm. M23358
18-26 The lintel over the icon frame south of the sanctuary. M23442

19

Kasim Ağa Mescidi

This mosque, located on the hill immediately to the southwest of the Odalar Camii, has been completely neglected since the fire of 1919, and what little remains of it today is used as a dwelling. The masonry of this building clearly labels it as Byzantine, but the site has never been studied. The only data we have on it are measurements made by the Eski Eserleri Koruma Encümeni, which are the basis of the plan published here. The interior of the building is a single, rectangular room roughly 8.10 by 9.60 meters, with entrances on all four sides, including a door to a groin-vaulted chamber to the east.

Schazmann visited the Kasim during his excavations of the Odalar Camii, and mentioned some frescoes; from these one can infer that the building was used for religious purposes, even though its plan does not suggest a church. Possibly it was a monastic structure, connected with the neighboring Odalar Camii. Evidently, however, it was built later. The alternation of stone and brick in some of the voussoirs suggests a Palaeologan foundation.

Bibliography

P. Schazmann, "Die Grabung an der Odalar Camii in Konstantinopel," *AA* 50 (1935), 519.

19-1 The east end, from the southeast. M21206

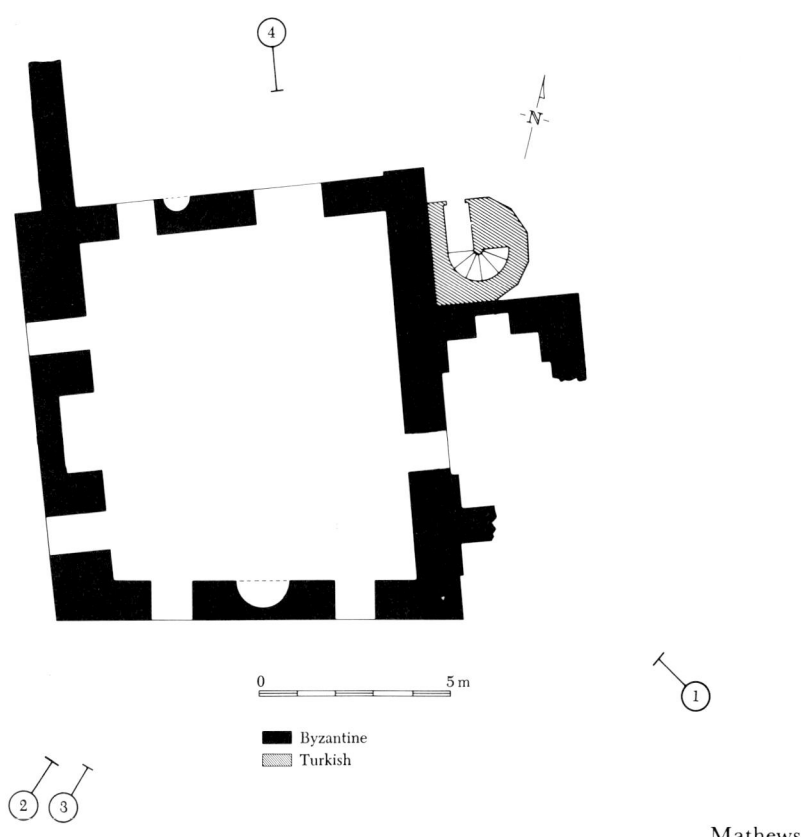

Mathews

19-2

19-3

188 Kasim Ağa Mescidi

19-2 View of the monument in its present state, from the southwest. M21160
19-3 General view from the southwest, with the Odalar Camii on the right, c. 1938. Photo German Archaeological Institute, Istanbul, 2699
19-4 View from the north, c. 1938. Photo German Archaeological Institute, Istanbul, 2698

19-4

20

Kefeli Mescidi

During the relocation of Christian communities from Caffa in the Crimea in 1475, this Byzantine monument, like the Odalar Camii, was given new Christian use under a second dedication, to St. Nicholas. Thereafter, it was used jointly by Catholics and Armenians. Not until 1629–30 was the building converted to a mosque; but in the meantime its Byzantine history was entirely lost, and speculation on its original dedication has thus far not yielded any positive results. Palazzo, who has written the history of the church in its second Christian phase, has demonstrated that it was not formerly the monastery of Manuēl, as Van Millingen and others believed; Janin is of the same opinion.

Grossmann, in his thorough examination of the structure, found evidence of a triple-nave layout which had escaped Van Millingen's attention. The building is of interest, therefore, as an example of a later Byzantine way of handling the ancient basilica form, even though it is not a work of great architectural merit nor a well-preserved monument. Of the west aisle (the apse points north), only the end walls survive, and the east aisle has disappeared entirely. An unusual inconsistency can be noted in the arcading between the flanking aisles and the central nave. The spacing of the arches is both irregular and unmatched from one side to the other, and the arches do not line up with the windows of the clerestory.

In view of the lack of firmly dated material for comparison, Grossmann's ninth century dating on the basis of masonry can hardly be accepted as secure. The many-faceted apse is a feature that belongs in the twelfth century or later, and the niches inside the apse correspond, among Constantinopolitan churches, only to those of the Palaeologan foundation, the Panagiotissa.

Bibliography

Van Millingen, *Byzantine Churches*, pp. 253–61.

B. Palazzo, *Deux anciennes églises dominicaines à Stamboul, Odalar Djami et Kefeli Mescidi* (Istanbul, 1951).

P. Grossmann, "Beobachtungen an der Kefeli-Mescid in Istanbul," *IM* 16 (1966), 241–49.

Janin, *La géographie*, pp. 320–22, 584.

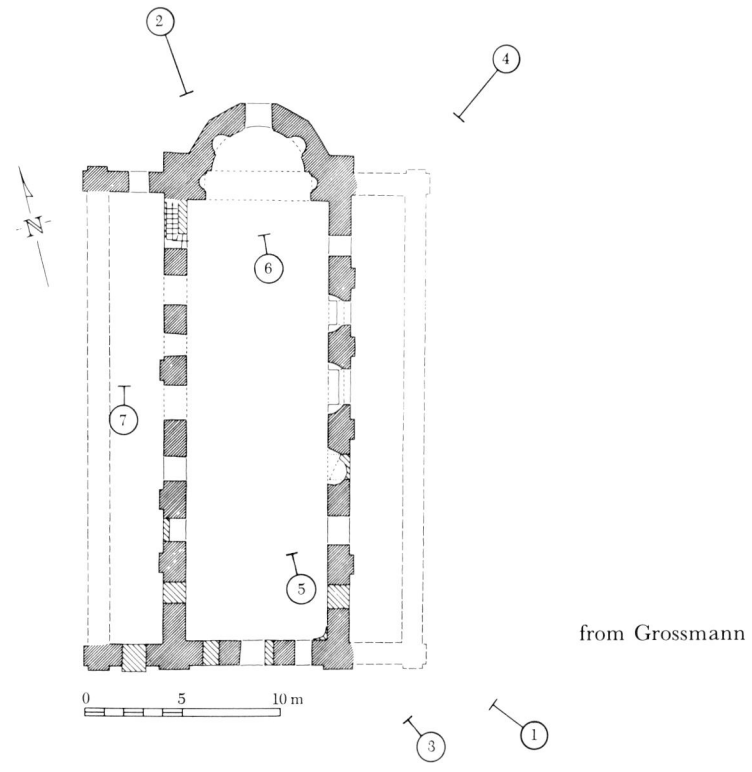

20-1 General view from the southeast (the apse points north), with the Chōra to the left, c. 1925. Photo A.K. Porter Collection, 5425, the Fogg Art Museum, Harvard University

20-2

20-3

20-4

20-2 The apse end. M23216
20-3 The south façade. M23213
20-4 The east flank of the church. Photo Grossmann, German Archaeological Institute, Istanbul, 66.125

20-5

20-6

20-7

20-5 The nave, viewed from the south, during the repairs of 1971. M23006
20-6 The apse during the repairs of 1971. M23020
20-7 The west aisle during the repairs of 1971. M23018

21

Manastır Mescidi

This much-mutilated church near the ancient Romanos Gate was studied cursorily by Van Millingen, who accepted it at face value, as a simple, single-naved building with a narthex to the west. It was still regarded this way by Eyice as recently as 1963, when he published his study of Palaeologan architecture. A valuable excavation by Pasadaios, however, carried out during the extension of the Millet Caddesi, revealed evidence of a more complex plan. Inside the east end of the structure Pasadaios found the lower courses of walls which had formerly, in traditional fashion, divided the sanctuary in three, and further down the nave he was able to trace foundation walls along the same lines in an east-west direction, obviously meant to support columns. Outside, to the north, west, and south, Pasadaios excavated the foundations of a surrounding porch, whose groin-vaulted covering left traces still visible in the church's exterior walls.

The present mosque structure bears few signs of its former Christian use. It does, however, retain one noteworthy original feature—a triple arcade between nave and narthex that gives an unusual openness to the interior space. The reconstruction of the original elevation is still problematical, but a quincunx plan seems more plausible than Pasadaios' suggestion of a vaulted basilica along the lines of Kastorian "folk" architecture; the delicate, multifaceted apses bear no relation to the style of Macedonia, whereas they fit nicely into the picture of Palaeologan design in Constantinople. As to the church's dedication, Janin leaves open a possible identification as the early fourteenth century foundation, Theotokos of Hag. Mēnodōra, Nymphodōra kai Metrodōra.

Bibliography

Van Millingen, *Byzantine Churches*, pp. 262–64.

Eyice, *Son devir Bizans Mimarisi*, pp. 26–28.

A. Pasadaios, *Epi dyo byzantinōn mnēmeiōn tēs Kōnstantinoupoleōs agnōstou onomasias* (Athens, 1965).

Janin, *La géographie*, pp. 319, 336, 544.

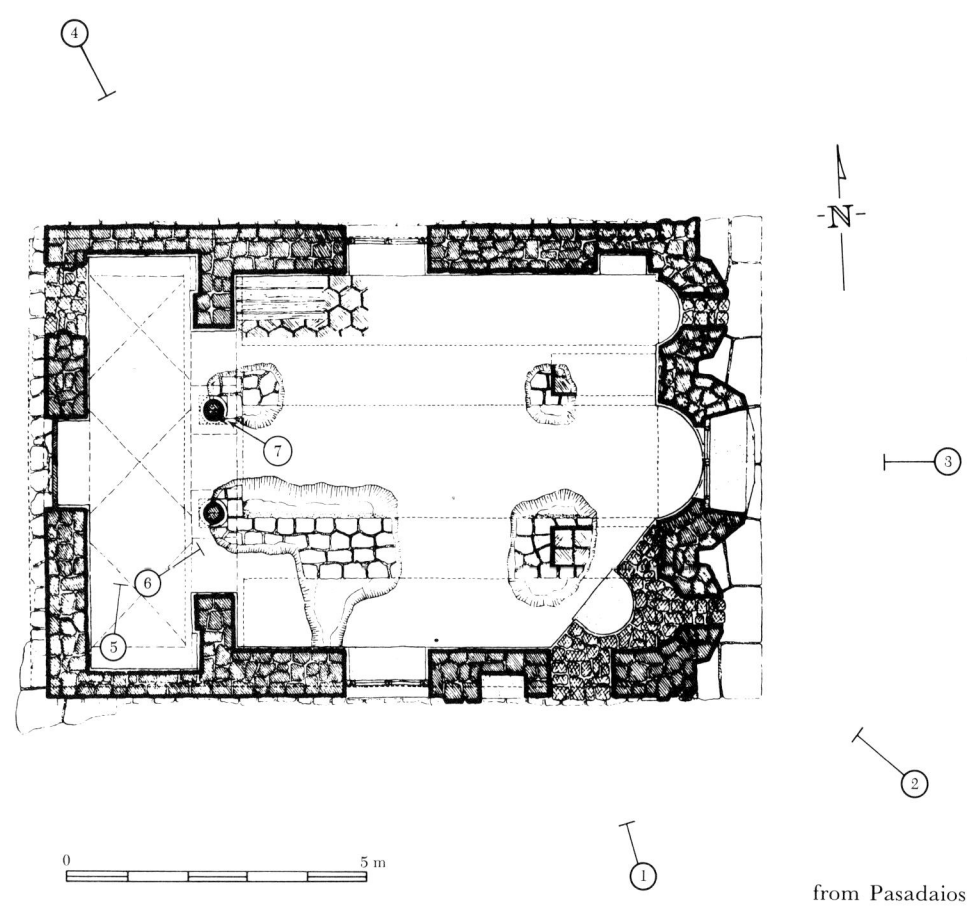

from Pasadaios

21-1

21-2

21-3

21-4

21-1   The south flank of the church, c. 1925. Photo Sender, rephotographed. M22501A
21-2   View from the southeast. M22154
21-3   The east end. M20319
21-4   The north flank of the church. M20325

21-5

198 Manastır Mescidi

21-6

21-7

21-5 The narthex viewed from the south. M22108
21-6 View from the narthex into the nave. M22118
21-7 The north capital in the narthex. M22140

22

Mangana (Arsenal) Churches

During the Allied occupation of Istanbul after the First World War, French forces, garrisoned between the Topkapı Sarayı and the Marmara, discovered a series of ruins while looking for a cellar to store their wine in. The subsequent excavation, which lasted intermittently for two years, was conducted by a Captain Blanc and was largely non-professional, though Demangel joined the staff as technical adviser in its second year. The identification of three monuments as Christos ho Philanthrōpos, Hag. Geōrgios tōn Manganōn, and Theotokos tōn Hodēgōn is therefore based less on archaeological than on general topographical information which is, as often, imprecise. The only secure name for the monuments, then, is the Byzantine name of the entire district as "ta mangana" or "the arsenal." After the excavation the site was abandoned and then put to use again as a Turkish military depot, precluding further study.

Demangel's identification of the monument closest to the sea as Christos ho Philanthrōpos rests on its proximity to a little hagiasma 60 meters to the south in the Sea Wall, which a continuous tradition down to the nineteenth century had associated with the monastery of the Philanthrōpos. However, nothing survives except substructures. The archaeological evidence is insufficient to indicate the position or plan of a church over the substructures, or, for that matter, whether it was a church at all. The suggested reconstruction made by Wulzinger is one of pure fancy, and his report, which anticipated that of Demangel, is highly inaccurate. If the colorful façade of the substructures is to be associated with the monastery of the Philanthrōpos, then it should not be attributed to Alexius I Comnenus (1081–1118), as Demangel proposed, but to the rebuilding of the monastery which Laurent attributes to Irene, daughter-in-law of Andronicus II, shortly after 1308. The extensive vocabulary of brickwork patterns here—meanders, interlace and basket-weave, beads, rosettes, lozenges, hearts, and sunbursts—finds its closest parallel in the south Lips church.

The second ruin, located across the railroad to the north of the first, shows better evidence of a church plan, apparently an ambulatory design, whose 10-meter dome would have been among the largest in the city. Topographical information locates the church of Hag. Geōrgios tōn Manganōn by the sea near Philanthrōpos, and the recessed brickwork of this ruin would agree with the erection of Hag. Geōrgios by Constantine Monomachus (1042–55). But the evidence is scarcely conclusive, even though Janin accepts it. Unfortunately, the only photographic documentation is a few photos in Demangel's publication.

The third monument was the best preserved, with some walls standing as much as 2 meters at the time of its excavation. Located further back from the Sea Wall, about 250 meters southwest of the so-called Philanthrōpos site, it followed a niched hexagonal plan very like the plan of Hag. Euphēmia. The original building dated from the fifth century, the semicircular court in front of it from a later building phase. On the level of the second building phase there was found directly in the center of the building a large dodecagonal marble font, originally with a baldachino, with steps descending into six niches inside. Beneath this the excavators discovered an octagonal brick font of the fifth century phase. This unique feature is the only evidence of the building's use; typical of the way the excavation was conducted, the eastern apse, which should have been the most important, was left unexcavated.

Schneider proposed that the monument be interpreted as a bath building, but the building lacks hypocausts and the other appurtenances of baths; and religious objects among the small finds of the site and the baldachino over the font leave us no other interpretation than that of Diehl and the excavators: we are dealing with a large hagiasma or holy font, of which there were many in ancient Constantinople. It should probably be identified, therefore, as the hagiasma of the monastery of Theotokos tōn Hodēgōn. A sanctuary housing the famous icon of the Hodēgētria was founded by the empress Pulcheria in the Mangana section in the mid-fifth century. The history of the prominent monastery associated with the shrine has been summarized by Janin.

Bibliography

C. Diehl, "Les fouilles du corps d'occupation français à Constantinople," *Académie des inscriptions et belles-lettres, Comptes rendues* (1922), 198–207; 1923, 241–48.

K. Wulzinger, *Byzantinische Baudenkmäler zu Konstantinopel auf der Seraispitze, die Nea, das Tekfur-serai und das Zisternenproblem* (Hanover, 1925), pp. 4–51.

V. Laurent, "Une princesse byzantine au cloître," *EO* 29 (1930), 29–60.

Schneider, *Byzanz,* pp. 59, 74–76, 90–91.

R. Demangel and E. Mamboury, *Le quartier des Manganes et la première région de Constantinople* (Paris, 1939).

Janin, *La géographie,* pp. 70–76, 199–207, 527–29.

22-1 Façade of substructures in the Sea Wall. M22818

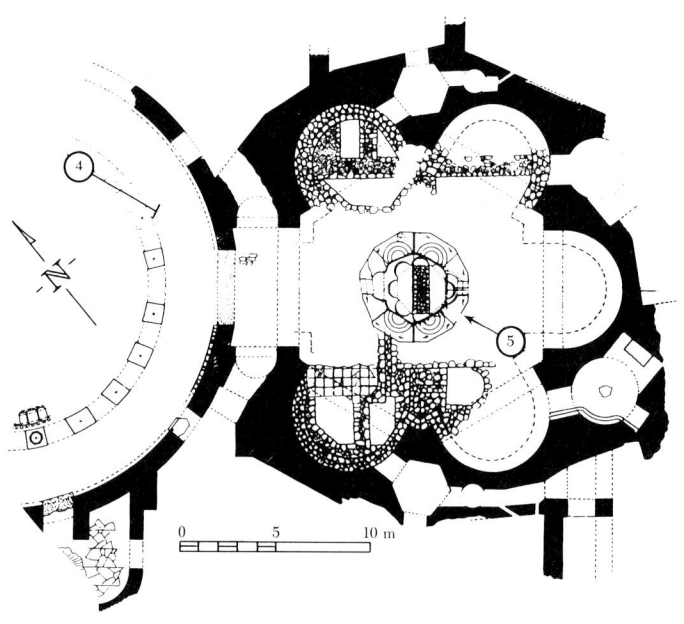

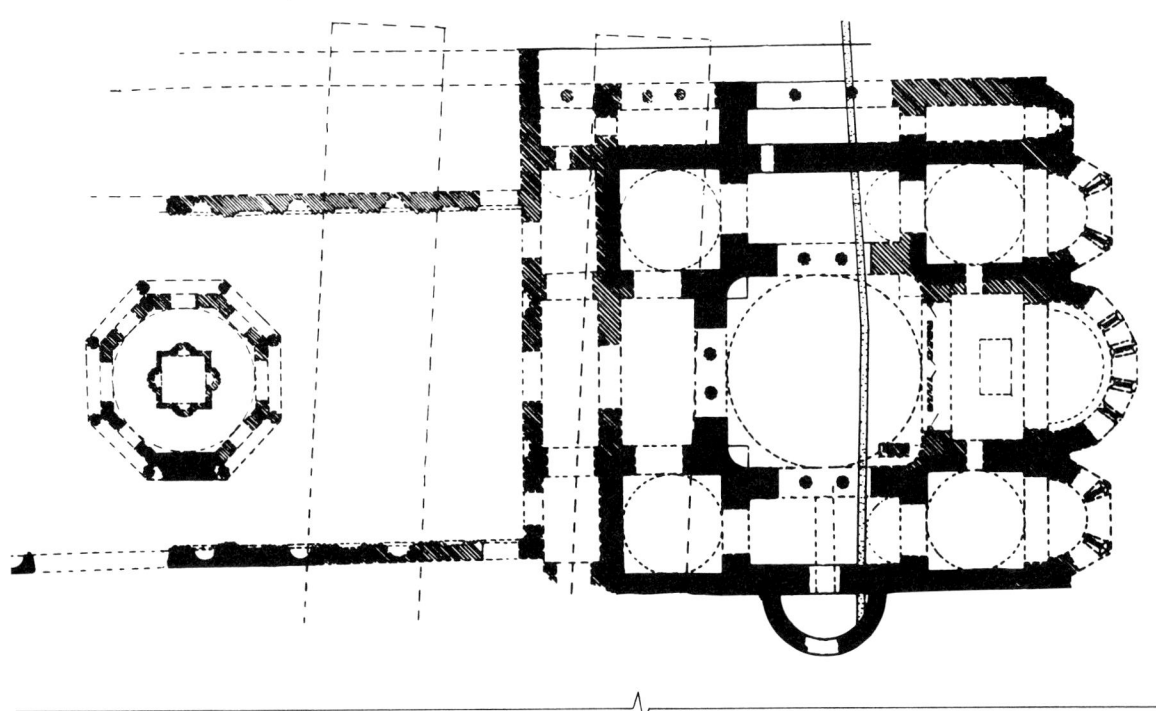
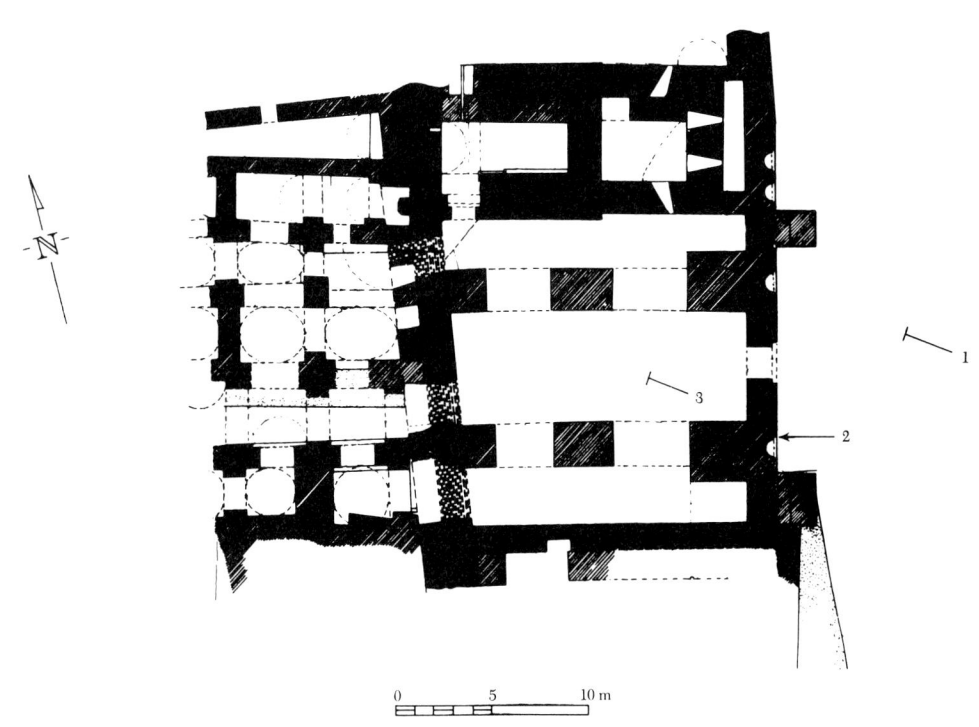

from Demangel

Mangana Churches

22-2

22-3

22-4

22-5

22-2 Detail of the decorative brickwork in the façade. M22844
22-3 Main, barrel-vaulted substructure of the so-called Philanthrōpos church. M25818
22-4 The hagiasma, general view from the north, c. 1940. Photo German Archaeological Institute, Kb3138
22-5 The font of the hagiasma, c. 1935. Photo Artamonoff, Dumbarton Oaks Field Committee, RA97a

23

Hag. Mēnas

In 1935 Schneider discovered, underneath the nineteenth century Greek church of Hag. Mēnas, the substructure of an early Byzantine church whose masonry appeared to be of the fifth century. The modern Hag. Mēnas, which is located in the ancient Psamathia section in the southwest part of the city, is known to have been preceded by a church on the same site dedicated to Hag. Polykarpos. Schneider thought he detected in the latter name a corruption of an earlier dedication to Hag. Karpos and Papylos, a church placed by Byzantine sources in this general area. However, Schneider's etymological connection is very tenuous, and the Byzantine topographical information, as Janin points out, is imprecise on the location of Karpos and Papylos. The original identity of the monument, therefore, is still a mystery.

Equally problematical is the function originally served by the remaining substructure. It consists basically of a broad, low hemisphere, ringed by a barrel-vaulted corridor and opening eastward through a low arch into an apsed chamber. Schneider suggested it was a martyrium crypt, housing the martyrs' tombs, but there is no archaeological evidence to support this contention. The lack of adequate access, the absence of windows except in the apse, and the massiveness of the construction all seem to imply, rather, that it was intended simply as foundation work. At some stage, perhaps after the ruin of the upper portion of the building, the substructure might have been adapted for use as a church proper; Janin reported evidence, in the center of the dome, of a Pantokratōr fresco not noted by Schneider.

Whatever the proper identification and function of this monument, which presently serves as a carpenter's shop, it is a structure of significance to Byzantine architectural history. From the plan of the substructure it can be supposed that the original superstructure was a rotunda with an ambulatory, a building type otherwise unknown in Constantinople.

Bibliography

Schneider, *Byzanz*, pp. 1-4.

R. Janin, "La topographie de Constantinople byzantine: études et découvertes, 1918-1938," *EO* 38 (1939), 145-46.

Janin, *La géographie*, p. 279.

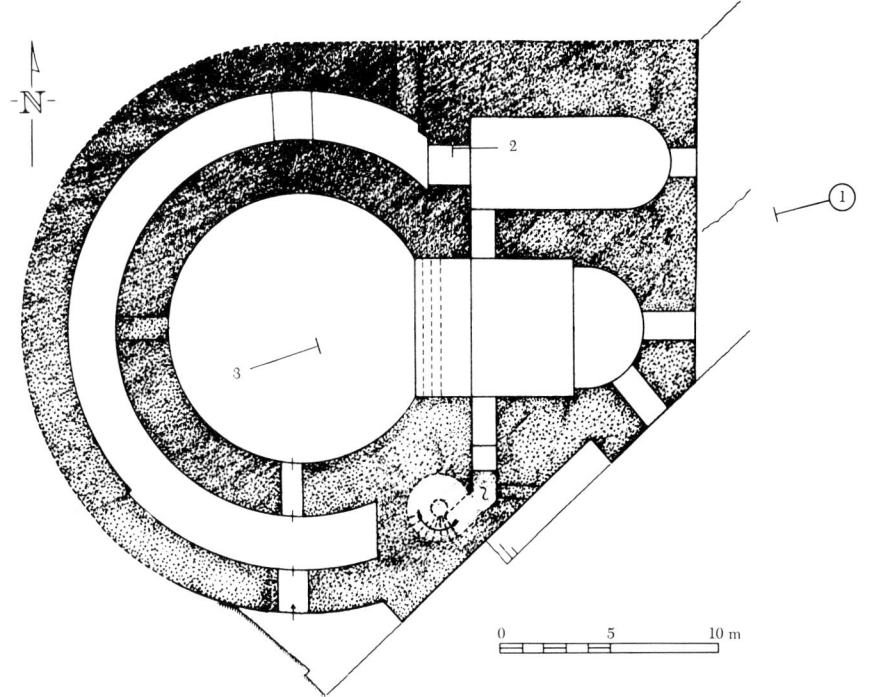

from Schneider

23-1 General view of the site from the east. M13706A

23-2

23-2 The northern portion of the ambulatory corridor, from the east, c. 1936. Photo Artamonoff, Dumbarton Oaks Field Committee, RA251b

23-3 View into the apse, c. 1936. Photo Artamonoff, Dumbarton Oaks Field Committee, RA251a

23-3

24

Myrelaion (The Place of Myrrh). Budrum Camii. Mesihpaşa Camii.

Erected between 920 and 922 by the upstart emperor Romanus Lecapenus alongside his new palace, this monastic church is one of the earliest cross-in-square or quincunx plans in the capital. Unfortunately, the Myrelaion has suffered considerable damage and disfigurement during its lifetime. Transformed into a mosque under Beyazit II (1481–1512), it was ravaged by fire in 1784 and again in 1912. Finally, and most disastrously of all, the building was heavily restored by the Istanbul Archaeological Museum in 1964–65. The restoration involved a refacing of 90 percent of the building's masonry with new concrete bricks, which revised window and door lines, erased masonry joints, and eliminated the delicate sawtoothed courses that had defined the original lines of the building. The project of restoration, however, was broken off before completion, leaving the church without windows, doors, flooring, or roofing, and no record was made of the alterations. Any observations of the architecture now, therefore, must be checked against photographs that antedate the restoration.

Archaeological reporting on the Myrelaion has been incomplete and uneven. The surveys of Van Millingen and Ebersolt were both conducted while the building was in active use as a mosque, and were thus necessarily hampered. After the ruin of the mosque, Talbot Rice, on the basis of a partial excavation, reported his conclusion that the church proper belonged to the eleventh century, while its substructure, which duplicates the plan of the church above, was a seventh century foundation. Both this theory and the hypothesis made by Bals—that the building was of a funerary type with crypt below and church above—were laid to rest by Striker's careful excavation of the substructure in 1965. Striker established that in spite of the differences in masonry between the upper and lower churches, the two are strictly contemporary. Pottery finds made in the excavation also led Striker to confirm both the tenth century dating and the attribution to Lecapenus proposed by earlier scholars. Striker has further demonstrated that the original function of the lower church was not religious but purely pragmatic, simply serving to raise the building to the level of the neighboring palace. Stratigraphical study revealed that the space remained unused until Palaeologan times. Evidently the Palaeologan period was also the time of repairs made after the fire of the Fourth Crusade; at this time revisions were made in the fenestration both of the main apse and of the north and south crossarms.

The Myrelaion was clearly an important and finely decorated building in its time. It was once richly finished in mosaics and marble revetments, with marble columns supporting the vaulting. All these decorative elements disappeared with the building's conversion to a mosque; but the stripped vaults, which retain their original delicacy, have miraculously survived.

Bibliography

Van Millingen, *Byzantine Churches,* pp. 196–200.

Ebersolt and Thiers, *Les églises,* pp. 139–46.

David Talbot Rice, "Excavations at Bodrum Camii, 1930," *Byzantion* 8 (1933), 151–76.

G. Balş, "Contribution à la question des églises superposées dans le domaine byzantin," *Actes du IVe Congrès international des études byzantines* (*Bulletin de l'institut archéologique bulgare* 10) 2, Sofia, 1936, pp. 156–67.

C.L. Striker, "A New Investigation of the Bodrum Camii and the Problem of the Myrelaion," *Istanbul Arkeoloji Müzeleri Yilliği* 13–14 (1966), 210–15.

R. Naumann, "Ausgrabungen bei der Bodrum Camii (Myrelaion)," *Istanbul Arkeoloji Müzeleri Yilliği* 13–14 (1966), 135–39.

R. Naumann, "Der antike Rundbau beim Myrelaion und der Palast Romanos I Lekapenos," *IM* 16 (1966), 199–216.

C.L. Striker, "The Myrelaion (Budrum Camii) in Istanbul," Ph.D. diss., the Institute of Fine Arts, New York University, 1968.

Janin, *La géographie,* pp. 351–54.

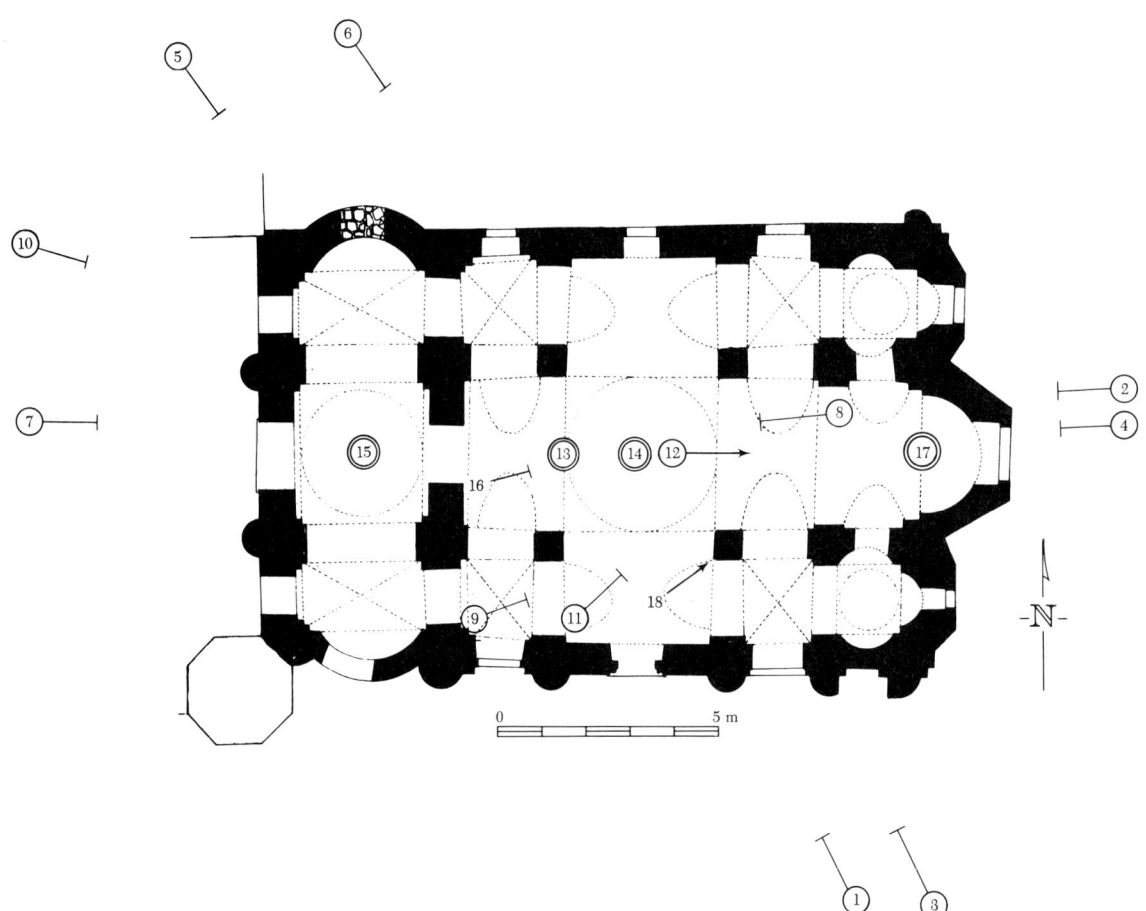

from Ebersolt

24-1 General view of the south flank, 1938. Photo R. Van Nice

24-2

24-2 General view from the east, c. 1925. Photo Eski Eserleri Koruma Encümeni, 258, Istanbul Archaeological Museum
24-3 Detail of the south flank at present. M17218
24-4 The east end at present. M17206

24-3

24-4

212   Myrelaion

24-5

24-6

24-5 General view from the northwest. M6834
24-6 The north flank, c. 1940. Photo Schneider, German Archaeological Institute, Istanbul, 01260A

24-7

- 24-7 The west façade at present. M4324
- 24-8 View from the sanctuary. M6632
- 24-9 View from the southwest bay. M6626A
- 24-10 The west façade, c. 1925. Photo A.K. Porter Collection, 1195, the Fogg Art Museum, Harvard University
- 24-11 The sanctuary, c. 1925. Photo A.K. Porter Collection, 5530, the Fogg Art Museum, Harvard University

24-8

24-9

24-10

24-11

24-12 The sanctuary at present. M6633A

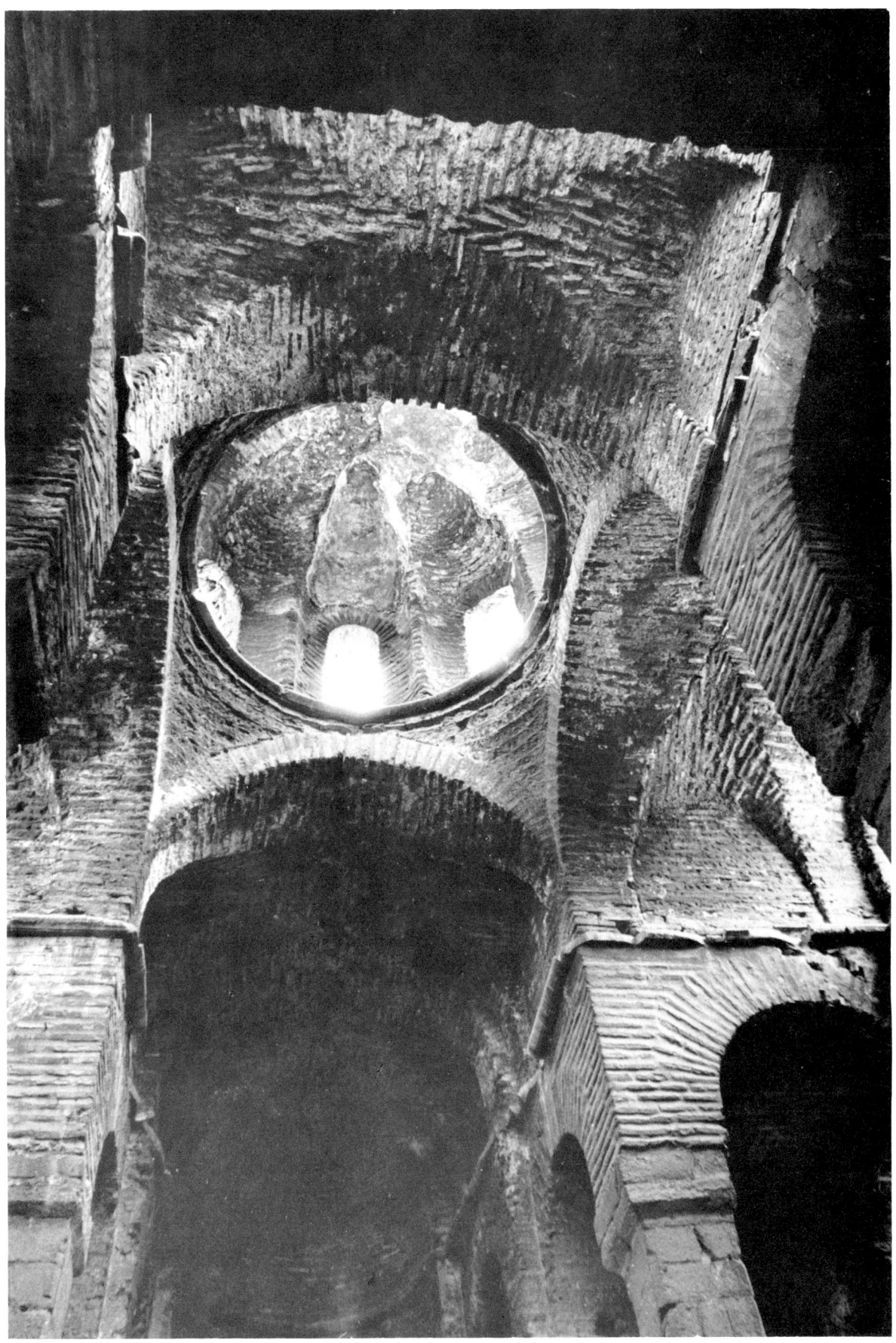

24-13 General view of the vaulting, with the east below. M10317

24-14

24-15

-17

24-16

24-18

24-14 The vaulting of the cupola and crossarms, with the east at the right. M10312
24-15 The vaulting of the narthex, viewed from the south. M6623A
24-16 The lower church, viewed from the west. M6703A
24-17 Vaulting of the apse. M10307
24-18 Southeast capital in the lower church. M6701A

25

Odalar Camii. Kemankeş Kara Mustafa Paşa Camii.

This monument was one of two Byzantine churches made over for Catholic use in 1475, when a community of Genoese from the Crimea resettled in Istanbul. For a century and a half thereafter, the church was served by the Dominicans under the name St. Mary of Constantinople. The original name of the monument, meanwhile, like that of the second church, the Kefeli, has been lost. Palazzo has suggested a dedication to Theotokos Kecharitomenē, and Janin has proposed Theotokos ta Kellaraias, but in neither case is the topographical information sufficient to yield more than hypotheses.

When the building was transformed into a mosque in 1640, it of course assumed the official name of the new founder, Kemankeş Paşa. Popularly, however, it became known as the Odalar Camii, or "chambers" mosque, named for the multiple compartments making up its substructure. The mosque fell into ruin in the 1890s, leaving only an exterior shell which was further devastated in the great fire of 1919.

It is clear from the recessed brick masonry still observable in the ruins of the Odalar that the building is of eleventh or twelfth century origin. Evidently the substructure of nineteen chambers represents a device for situating the church securely on a steep incline. The first archaeologist to report on the site was Mamboury, who made only preliminary observations of the monument. Several years later, Brunov and Alpatov undertook a more serious investigation, Brunov drawing up the only plan, however inadequate, that has been done on the Odalar to date. The plan indicated a quincunx of generous dimensions, with an interior width of about 11 meters. The south flanking apse was discovered to be wider than the north, creating a chapel that projected southward beyond the line of the exterior wall; and in this chapel Alpatov reported frescoes depicting the Life of the Virgin and the Infancy. Along the north side of the church Brunov's plan noted an outside aisle which was entered by a stairway on the east.

Schazmann, working in the 1930s, carried study on this monument somewhat further by partially excavating the site and surveying the substructure. Underneath the chambered level Schazmann discovered earlier foundations which he conjectured were of seventh century construction. The chambers themselves, he determined, even though their purpose was structural, had been used for burials and were once decorated with frescoes. A number of these frescoes still exist, having been rescued and removed to the Istanbul Archaeological Museum; a Palaeologan relief from the site has recently been discussed by Belting. Meanwhile the site itself has continued to disintegrate rapidly with the encroachment of new houses and apartment buildings around it.

Bibliography

E. Mamboury, "Autour d'Odalar-Djamissi, à Stamboul," *EO* 19 (1920), 69–73.

N. Brunov, "Die Odalar-Djami von Konstantinopel," *BZ* 26 (1926), 352–72.

M. Alpatov, "Die Fresken der Odalar-Djami in Konstantinopel," *BZ* 26 (1926), 373–79.

P. Schazmann, "Die Grabung an der Odalar Camii in Konstantinopel," *AA* 50 (1935), 511–19.

P. Schazmann, "Des fresques byzantines récentement découvertes par l'auteur dans les fouilles à Odalar Camii, Istanbul," *Atti del V congresso internazionale di studi byzantini* 2 (Rome, 1936), 371–86.

R. Janin, "La topographie de Constantinople byzantine: études et découvertes, 1918–38," *EO* 38 (1939), 141–42.

B. Palazzo, *Deux anciennes églises dominicaines à Stamboul, Odalar Djami et Kefeli Medsjidi* (Istanbul, 1951).

Janin, *La géographie,* pp. 188, 583.

H. Belting, "Zur Skulptur aus der zeit um 1300 in Konstantinopel," *Münchener Jahrbuch der Bildenden Kunst* 23 (1972), 3, 63–100.

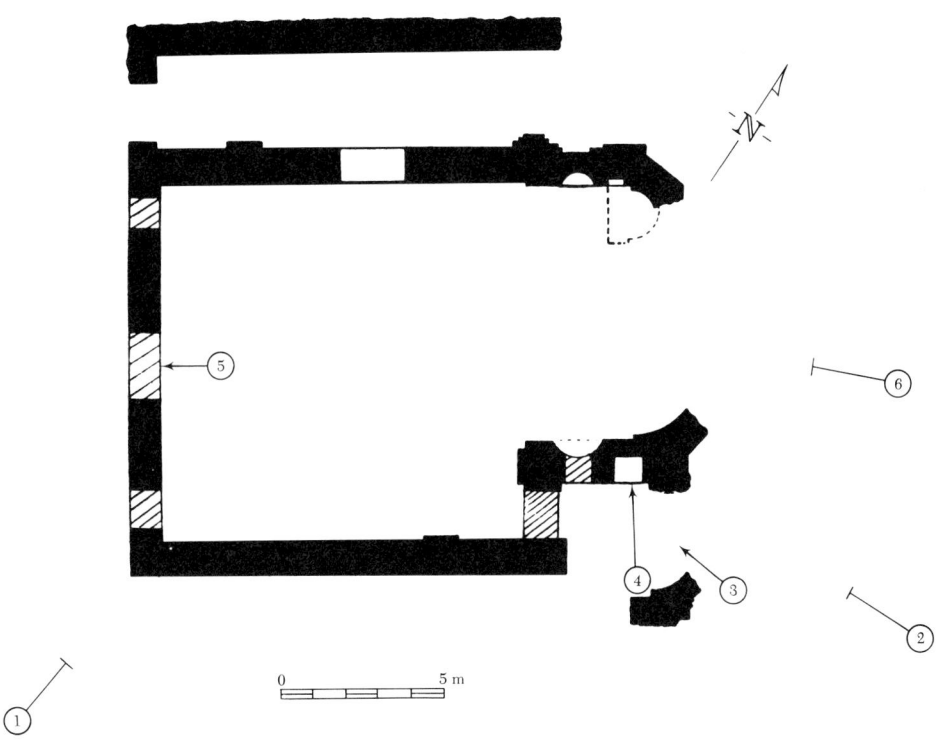

from Brunov

25-1

25-1 General view from the northwest, from the minaret of the Kasim Ağa Mescidi, 1933. Photo Eski Eserleri Koruma Encümeni, 865, Istanbul Archaeological Museum
25-2 View of the east end and the substructures of the church, c. 1925. Photo Sender, rephotographed. M22516A
25-3 The southeast chapel, 1933. Photo Eski Eserleri Koruma Encümeni, 847, Istanbul Archaeological Museum

25-2

25-3

25-4

25-5

25-4 Detail of the masonry in the southeast chapel, 1933. Photo Eski Eserleri Koruma Encümeni, 842, Istanbul Archaeological Museum

25-5 Detail of the masonry over the west entrance, viewed from the east. M21242

25-6 View of the site from the east at present, with the interior of the north wall at right. M21254

25-6

26

Hag. Polyeuktos (St. Polyeuktus)

In 1960 two fragments of an inscription that came to light beside the Atatürk Bulvarı were identified by Mango and Ševčenko as belonging to the dedicatory inscription of Hag. Polyeuktos. This discovery fixed a new locus in the topography of Constantinople, the site of the splendid church built in 524–27 by the wealthy aristocrat Anicia Juliana, and marked the opening under Harrison and Fıratlı of a rather unexpected chapter in the history of Byzantine archaeology.

The excavation, reports of which have been published only in preliminary form to date, has revealed a massive platform of substructures. To the west, some 5 meters below the presumed level of the church's floor, lay a marble paved atrium which gave access on the basement level to a subnarthex corridor and a long passage leading east to a crypt beneath the sanctuary. The main floor of the church was reached by a broad stair ramp rising from the atrium to the narthex. The proportions of the building east of the narthex were nearly square, a generous 52 meters on a side. The foundations indicate a basilica kind of division of church space into a nave and flanking aisles, but the nave foundations are so massive that one is led to suppose masonry vaulting over the center of the church. Although nothing remained standing above the substructures, it is possible that the arrangement of the dedicatory inscription, which encircled the nave on a set of elaborately carved niches featuring peacocks, plus the evidence of fragments of fallen piers and cornices, will justify a reconstruction of some of the major features of the superstructure.

Even if such a reconstruction proves impossible, the extraordinary wealth of small finds at Hag. Polyeuktos makes it one of the most important excavations in Constantinople. The sixth century turns out to be much more complex than anticipated. The sculpture of niches, piers, capitals, and cornices displays a new, exuberant style of decoration, at times orientalizing in its motifs, that apparently had established itself alongside of, or in opposition to, the restrained and conservative Justinianic style. Vigorous and surprisingly naturalistic vine reliefs appear on the peacock niches, while strictly formalized plant designs of a heavy, sensuous character show up in piers and capitals. In addition, a set of figurative relief panels was found carrying busts of Christ, the Mother of God, and the Apostles. Their mutilation in iconoclast times attests the early date of the reliefs; if they belonged to the chancel enclosure they may provide us with our earliest instance of an iconostasis. Evidence of mosaic was found everywhere, including fragments of mosaic pavement. Harrison has identified dozens of different colored marbles used in inlay work, along with glass, mother-of-pearl, and gold. Apparently all this decoration was appreciated even centuries later, for when the church fell to ruin at the end of the twelfth century much of the sculpture was carried off for reuse elsewhere—at the Pantokratōr in Constantinople or San Marco in Venice.

The excavation of Hag. Polyeuktos in its expected final form will also yield an abundance of factual information of a much more prosaic nature, made possible by carefully controlled excavation procedures. Building methods and materials have been meticulously examined, and John W. Hayes, who contributed to the preliminary reports, has worked out the first systematic chronology of pottery in Constantinople from Roman times to modern Turkish times.

Bibliography

C. Mango and I. Ševčenko, "Remains of the Church of St. Polyeuktos at Constantinople," *DOP* 15 (1961), 243-47.

R.M. Harrison and N. Fıratlı, "Excavations at Saraçhane in Istanbul," *DOP* 19 (1965), 230-36; 20 (1966), 222-38; 21 (1967), 273-78; 22 (1968), 195-216.

Janin, *La géographie,* 405-6.

Mathews, *The Early Churches of Constantinople,* pp. 52-55.

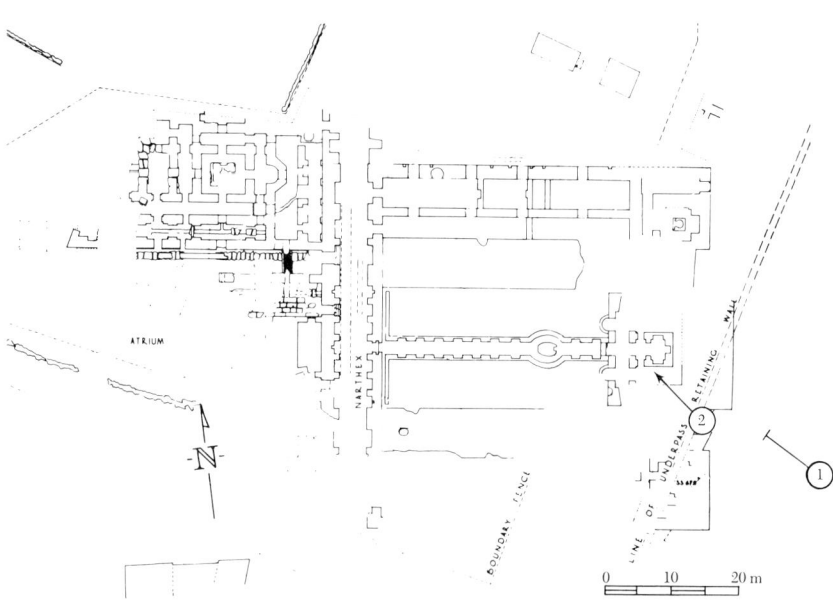

from Harrison

26-1

26-2

26-1 General view from the southeast at the end of digging in 1968. Photo R.M. Harrison
26-2 The crypt from the southeast. Photo R.M. Harrison

26-3

26-4

26-5

26-3 Pier capital with palm tree, no. 6876. Photo R.M. Harrison
26-4 Basket capital with split palmettes, no. 6288. Photo R.M. Harrison
26-5 Capital with lattice work. Photo R.M. Harrison
26-6 Engaged pier capital, no. 6843. Photo R.M. Harrison
26-7 Peacock niche with inscription, no. 849. Photo R.M. Harrison
26-8 Detail of peacock niche, now in the Istanbul Archaeological Museum. M16332

26-6

26-7

26-8

Hag. Polyeuktos 229

26-9

26-10

26-11

26-9   Wall panel with two decorated zones, no. 2712. Photo R.M. Harrison
26-10 Cornice with monograms, no. 3390. Photo R.M. Harrison
26-11 Detail of the cornice with monograms. Photo R.M. Harrison

27

Sancaktar Hayreddin Mescidi

Scholarly speculation on this Byzantine monument offers us a choice of dates that ranges over an entire millennium. The first attempt to date the church was made by Van Millingen, who tentatively suggested the fourteenth century; Janin proposed the eleventh or twelfth, and, finally, Pasadaios, who has made a recent and fairly detailed study of the site, has advanced a claim that it is of fourth to sixth century origin. This huge uncertainty, still unclarified, reflects the primitive state of our archaeological knowledge of the Sancaktar and the need for further research on the monument.

The history of the building from the Turkish Conquest onward is reasonably well known. Hayreddin, standard-bearer to Mehmet II, converted it to a mosque in the fifteenth century. The building remained a mosque until 1894, when it was ravaged by an earthquake, and since that time its shell has been occupied by dwellings. No actual excavation has been carried out on the church itself, but preparations for building an apartment complex to the south have recently exposed the foundations along that side.

The plan of the Sancaktar is fairly simple. The exterior was octagonal, while the interior consisted of a Greek cross formed by four shallow, barrel-vaulted crossarms. As archaeologists have long recognized, the apse was of different construction from the main part of the building. Van Millingen read this as evidence of the conversion of a secular building to church use; but Pasadaios inverted the sequence, supposing that the apse, which he ascribed to the fourth century, was older than the rest of the building.

Van Millingen's interpretation of the building sequence is the more convincing of the two; on the other hand, at least on the basis of what can be observed of the interior, Pasadaios' early dating is probably to be preferred. The massive tripling of arches over the crossarms on the inside is reminiscent of the masonry of the fourth century hippodrome, and the broad pendentives that link the arches with the dome are also characteristic of Early Byzantine style.

It is difficult to say at what point this powerfully built structure might have been converted into a church. The simple piers and capitals, while they are of early design, offer us no clues, as they might have been installed at any period. Similarly, Pasadaios' observation that the apse was rounded below the windows is not helpful as evidence; although he cited this in support of his early dating, it is a feature that can be noted as well at the Sekbanbaşı and at Iōannēs en tō Troullō, both eleventh or twelfth century churches.

Traditionally the Sancaktar has been identified with the monastery of the Gastria. Janin has endorsed this hypothesis, although there is no firm archaeological support for this identification, and the topographical evidence is very vague.

Bibliography

Van Millingen, *Byzantine Churches,* pp. 268–71.

A. Pasadaios, *Epi dyo byzantinōn mnēmeiōn tēs Kōnstantinoupoleōs agnōstou onomasias* (Athens, 1965), pp. 1–55.

Janin, *La géographie,* pp. 67–68.

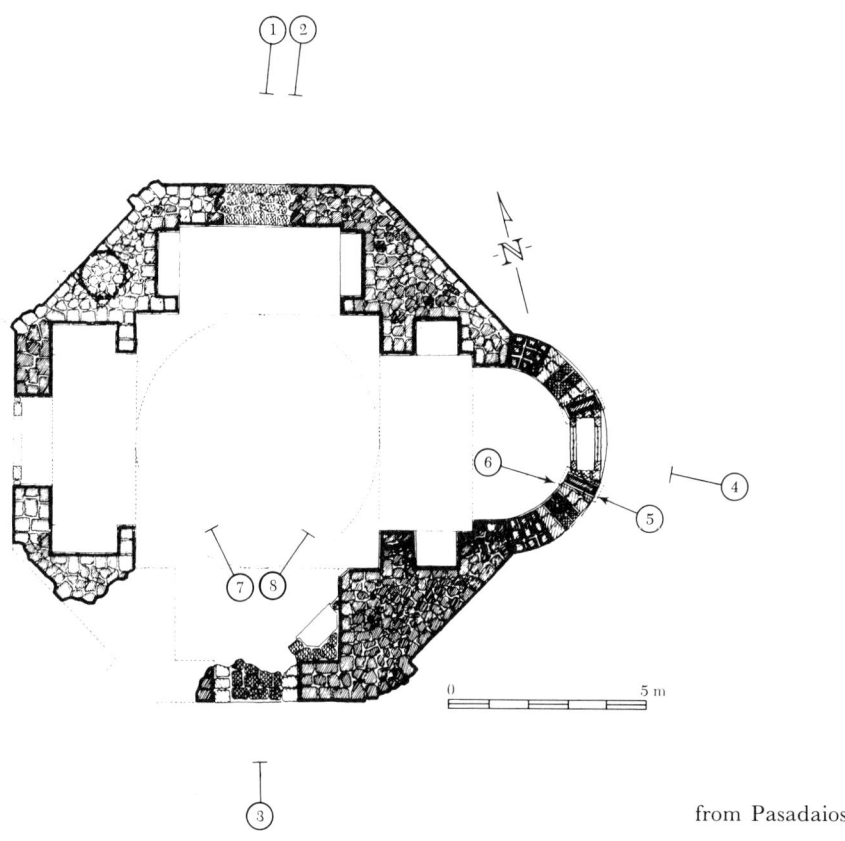

from Pasadaios

27-1

27-2

27-1 General view from the northwest at present. M21454
27-2 General view from the northwest, c. 1910. Photo Van Millingen, Burrows Library of Byzantine and Modern Greek, King's College, University of London

27-3

27-3 General view from the south. M13717
24 4 The east end. M13711
27-5 South capital in the apse, viewed from the outside. M13715
27-6 South pier and capital in the apse, viewed from the interior, c. 1925. Photo Sender, rephotographed. M22520

27-4

27-5

27-6

27-7

27-8

27-7 The barrel vaults of the west and north crossarms, viewed from the south. Photo A.K. Porter Collection, 1261, the Fogg Art Museum, Harvard University
27-8 The east barrel vault and adjoining pendentives, viewed from the southwest. M21472

28

Sekbanbaşı Mescidi

This small, stubby church, which was located just below the Valens Aqueduct, was made into a mosque in the fifteenth century. The building was abandoned at some time during the 1920s, and torn down in 1943 for the widening of Atatürk Bulvarı; the remaining foundations were then destroyed in 1952. Gurlitt described the building while it was still in use as a mosque, but his observations and plan are not very reliable. A more accurate plan was drawn up by Schneider in 1936, though by this time the narthex was missing. Schneider noted the recessed brick construction which dates the church to eleventh or early twelfth century.

The design of the east end with three apses rounded on the exterior links this church to Hag. Iōannēs en tō Troullō, but the interior plan finds no parallel in Constantinople. The plan should be reconstructed as a quincunx or cross-in-square to which the apses were added directly, without intervening sanctuary bays, giving the building its squat proportions. The sanctuary must have extended as far as the eastern pair of columns supporting the central dome. To find this plan in other Byzantine monuments one must look far afield, to Cappadocia or to the twelfth century Martorana in Palermo.

Earlier authors unanimously identified the Sekbanbaşı as the Church of Christos tēs Kyras Marthas, but this identification is no longer tenable. The topographical information on the Kyra Martha provided by historical sources has been more carefully studied by Janin and other scholars; and while there is disagreement as to that church's actual location, they have made clear that it cannot have been the Sekbanbaşı.

Bibliography

C. Gurlitt, *Die Baukunst Konstantinopels* (Berlin, 1912), p. 43.

Schneider, *Byzanz*, p. 61.

Janin, *La géographie*, pp. 324–26, 544.

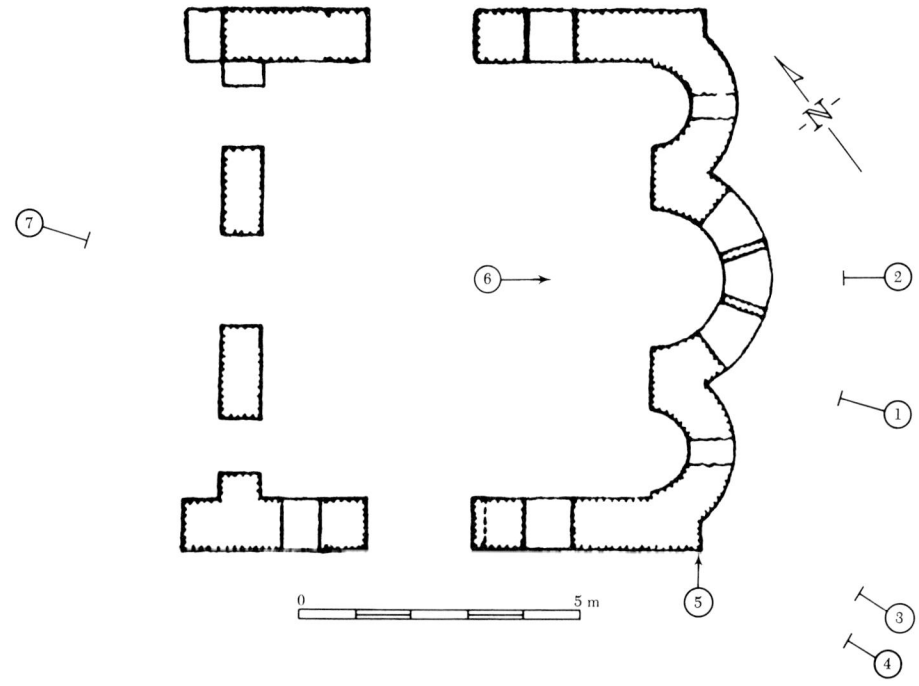

from Schneider

28-1

238 Sekbanbaşı Mescidi

28-2

28-1 General view from the east in 1877, from Paspatcs' lithograph
28-2 The east end, c. 1935. Photo Schneider, German Archaeological Institute, Istanbul, 2700

28-3

28-4

28-5

240   Sekbanbaşı Mescidi

28-3 View from the southeast, c. 1930. A.K. Porter Collection, 171.2,Is8,1, the Fogg Art Museum, Harvard University

28-4 View from the southeast, c. 1920. A.K. Porter Collection, 171.2,Is8,2Bal, the Fogg Art Museum, Harvard University

28-5 Detail of the masonry. Photo Schneider, German Archaeological Institute, Istanbul, 4470

28-6 The interior of the central apse, c. 1935. Photo Eski Eserleri Koruma Encümeni, 4008, Istanbul Archaeological Museum

28-7 The narthex, viewed from the west, c. 1935. Photo Eski Eserleri Koruma Encümeni, 3993, Istanbul Archaeological Museum

28-6

28-7

Sekbanbaşı Mescidi   241

29

Hag. Sergios kai Bakchos en tois Hormisdou (Sts. Sergius and Bacchus in the Palace of Hormisdas) and Hag. Petros kai Paulos (Sts. Peter and Paul). Küçük Ayasofya Camii.

Justinian's court historian, Procopius, describes this double church complex as a part of the palace and an ornament of the palace, a distinction which adds special interest to one of the most important monuments of Early Byzantine architecture. The Hormisdas palace, which lay along the Marmara below the Hippodrome, served Justinian as his private residence during the reign of his uncle Justin I, and upon ascending the throne he remodeled it and incorporated it into the Great Palace located further along the shore to the east. The historical sources indicate that Justinian erected the church of Hag. Petros kai Paulos here, commemorating his name-saint Peter, while he was still a private citizen, probably in the years 518–20. It was designed as a basilica, but nothing now remains of it except the broadly arched north wall which is preserved in the present south wall of Hag. Sergios kai Bakchos.

The church of Hag. Sergios kai Bakchos, on the other hand, stands substantially intact. It is true that windows and entrances have been modified, the floor level has risen, the interior has been plastered and painted, and a Turkish porch has been erected across the façade where formerly there was an atrium. Nevertheless, the fabric of the building, its fragile sixteen-sided dome over eight delicate niches, continues to defy all the shocks of history, including the passing of all of Istanbul's rail traffic within 5 meters of its south wall.

Erected between 527 and 536, Hag. Sergios kai Bakchos may be seen as the emperor's private version of that which he accomplished on monumental scale at Hagia Sophia. Designed as an octagon within a square, it exploits many of the same sophisticated effects that are used to such advantage in the Great Church: exedrae expanding the central nave on diagonal axes, colorful columns screening the ambulatories from the nave, and dramatically contrasted light and shadow playing on the deeply undercut sculpture of capitals and entablature. Whether the plan itself is to be linked to a whole tradition of octagonal palace churches, as proposed by Krautheimer, the aesthetic seems clearly to belong to a palace architectural tradition. Mango in a recent article tried to deny the palace associations of the church altogether by connecting it instead with strictly monastic use, and that Monophysite. The document appealed to, however, does not apply to Hag. Sergios kai Bakchos, as Janin had already concluded when he cited the document.

The continued use of the building as a mosque has so far prevented thorough archaeological study, and this is regrettable in view of the importance of the building to architectural history. Our best information on the building as a whole is still that contained in Ebersolt's survey over sixty years ago, though studies made since that time have filled in one or another detail of the picture. Underwood, basing his study on Ebersolt's plan, worked out the principles of measure underlying the design, units based on divisions of the 50-foot diameter of the dome; and Sanpaolesi has added precision to our knowledge of the shape of the dome, although in other respects his observations are not always reliable. More recently Feld has reported on the plaster decoration of the building, while my own study has tried to clarify the liturgical use of space in the church.

Bibliography

Van Millingen, *Byzantine Churches,* pp. 62–83.

Ebersolt and Thiers, *Les églises,* pp. 21–51.

C. Gurlitt, *Die Baukunst Konstantinopels* (Berlin, 1912), pp. 18–20.

P.A. Underwood, "Some Principles of Measure in the Architecture of the Period of Justinian," *CA* 3 (1948), 64–74.

P. Sanpaolesi, "La chiesa dei ss. Sergio e Bacco à Costantinopoli," *Rivista dell' istituto nazionale d'archeologia e storia dell' arte,* n.s. 10 (1961), 116–80.

Krautheimer, *Early Christian and Byzantine Architecture,* pp. 161–70.

Otto Feld, "Beobachtungen in der Küçük Ayasofya zu Istanbul," *IM* 18 (1968), 264–69.

Janin, *La géographie,* pp. 451–55.

Mathews, *The Early Churches of Constantinople,* pp. 42–51.

C. Mango, "The Church of Saints Sergius and Bacchus at Constantinople and the Alleged Tradition of Octagonal Palatine Churches," *Jahrbuch der österreichischen Byzantinistik* 21, *Festschrift für Otto Demus* (Vienna, 1972), 189–93.

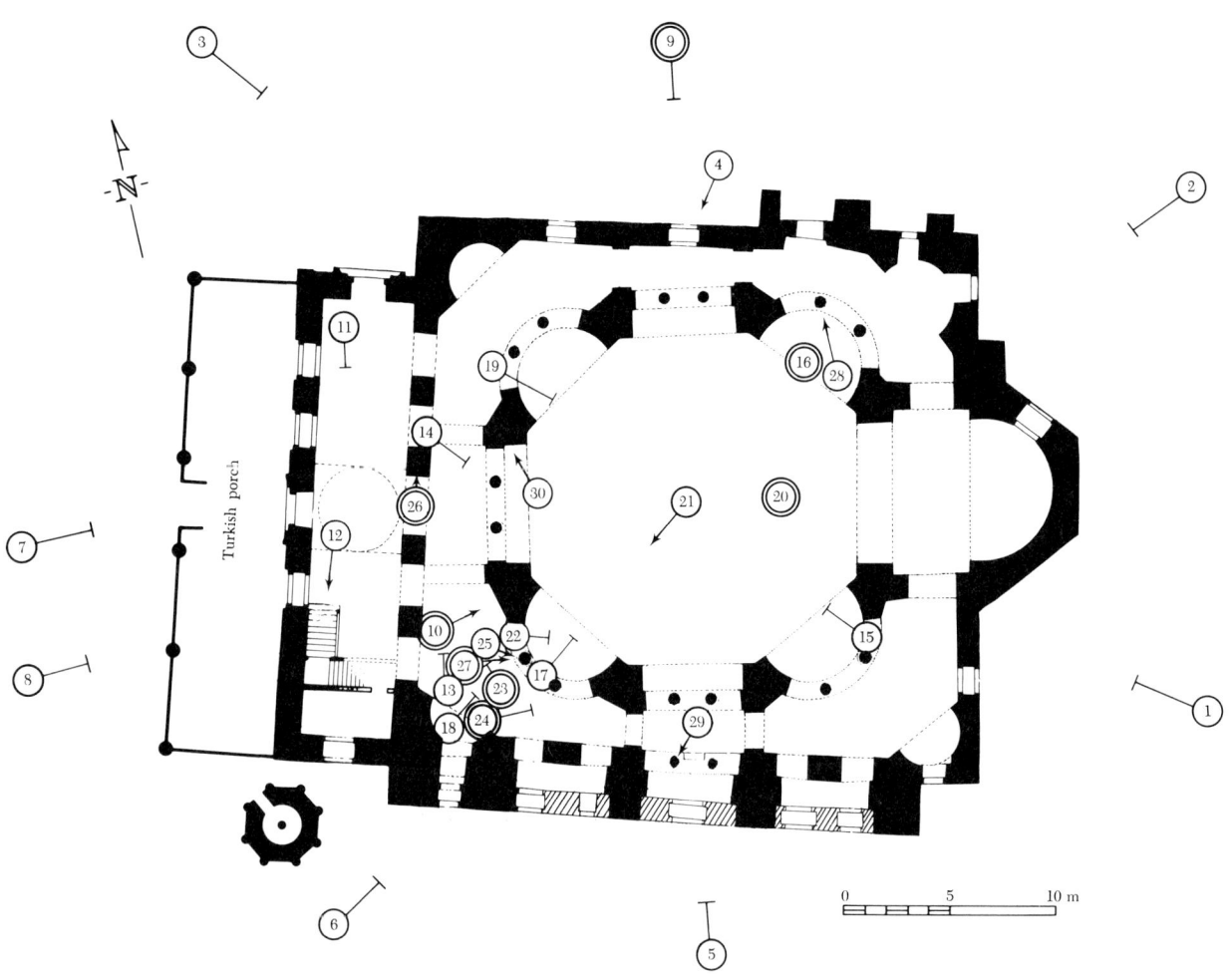

29-1 The east end of the church, 1950. Photo Josephine Powell, T 7–1

29-2

29-3

29-4

29-2 View from the northeast. M9117
29-3 The north flank seen from the northwest. M15313
29-4 Detail of the north flank showing filled-in arcade. M108

29-5

29-6

29-5 View from the south with remains of the Sea Wall in the foreground. M2624
29-6 The south flank, incorporating the north wall of Hag. Petros and Paulos. M2711

29-7

248   Hag. Sergios kai Bakchos en tois Hormisdou

29-8

29-9

29-7 The west facade in 1946. Photo Dumbarton Oaks Field Committee, c 46.4
29-8 The west facade. M2723A
29-9 The cupola from the north. M6615

29-10

29-11

29-10 South buttress on the west face of the cupola during repairs in 1946. Photo Dumbarton Oaks Field Committee, c 46.16

29-11 The narthex from the north. M6525

29-12

29-14

29-13

29-12 Decorative arch over the stair in the narthex. M15965
29-13 The western ambulatory from the south, with the narthex to the left. M6532
29-14 View from the western ambulatory into the nave. M6536

252 Hag. Sergios kai Bakchos en tois Hormisdou

29-16

29-15 General view of the interior from the southeast gallery. Photo Josephine Powell, T 7–7
29-16 The northeast niche. M15910

29-17

29-18

29-17   General view of the interior from the southwest gallery. M10414

29-18   The south ambulatory and a view of the nave from the southwest niche. Photo R. Hamann-MacLean, Bildarchiv Foto Marburg, 229150

29-19 The sanctuary and southeast niche. M25361

29-20

29-21

29-22

29-20 The eastern half of the dome. M25407
29-21 The southwest niche. M6603
29-22 The piers of the south side of the nave, from the southwest gallery. M15961

29-23

29-24

29-23 The gallery over the narthex from the south. M6828
29-24 The south gallery from the west. M6816

29-25

29-26

29-25 The north capital in the southwest niche, ground floor. M15917
29-26 The north capital in the gallery over the narthex. M10509
29-27 The north capital in the southwest niche, gallery level. M15929
29-28 The north capital in the northeast niche, ground floor. M6734
29-29 The west capital in the south bay of the south ambulatory. M10515
29-30 Detail of the entablature in the western niche. M6802

29-27

29-29

29-28

29-30

Hag. Sergios kai Bakchos en tois Hormisdou

30

Sinan Paşa Mescidi

In the middle of the last century, when Paspates visited this anonymous ruin not far from the Gül Camii, an apse was still largely intact. Now, however, only the substructure remains. The ruins indicate that this was a chapel, probably of a hall plan, measuring about 15 meters in length, but the site has never been studied nnr has any plan of the building ever been made.

Schneider, who saw the ruin in the 1930s, speculated on the basis of the masonry that this structure dated from the tenth or eleventh century. However, the close patterning of brick motifs is sufficiently similar to the masonry of the South Lips church so that we can more realistically date it in the Palaeologan period.

Bibliography

Paspates, *Byzantinai meletai*, p. 384.
Schneider, *Byzanz*, p. 72.

30-1 General view from the north in 1877, from Paspates' lithograph

30-2

30-3

30-2 General view from the north, c. 1935. German Archaeological Institute, Istanbul, 2747

30-3 The east end at present. M21956

Sinan Paşa Mescidi 261

31

Hagia Sophia (Holy Wisdom). Ayasofya Camii. Ayasofya Müzesi.

The Old Hagia Sophia

The existing church of Hagia Sophia was preceded on the same site by an earlier cathedral that had two building phases: dedicated under Constantius in 360, the building was rebuilt after a fire in 404 and reconsecrated in 415 under Theodosius II. Despite the importance of this church as the cathedral of the capital, it is poorly known in both phases; the archaeological evidence which exists is slight, and even that has been inadequately studied.

Only two parts of the old Hagia Sophia are accessible to archaeologists. The skeuophylakion, still standing at the northeast corner of the present church, was reported on by Dirimtekin, but he did little besides confirm the long-standing supposition of its pre-Justinianic date. No accurate plan was drawn up, and no excavation was made to discover the building's exact date. Changes in the masonry that can be observed inside the lower parts of this structure suggest, in fact, that it may belong to more than one building phase. Literary sources, upon which archaeologists must rely heavily in any study of the old Hagia Sophia, give us the only other information we have on the skeuophylakion; they are fairly consistent in identifying the building as a repository for sacred vessels and the starting point for the procession of the Entrance of the Mysteries in the liturgy.

The remains of an impressive entranceway, which Schneider excavated in the atrium, also belong to the pre-Justinianic church. Schneider believed this huge, porticoed structure to belong to the original church façade, but literary sources suggest instead that it be identified with the propylaeum that preceded the atrium of the church. Indeed, the extraordinary length of the stoa makes this solution the only plausible one. The sculptural material from the propylaeum clearly belongs to the Theodosian reconstruction of 404-15, and is the finest work of that period in Constantinople.

Concerning the body of the church itself, archaeology tells us nothing, and literary sources, which were first reviewed by Millet, provide us with only sparse details of the plan. Evidently the building was a galleried basilica preceded by an atrium. The interior was magnificently furnished, with an altar of gold and, in the center, a lofty ambo. Outside, sources tell us, a baptistery stood near the skeuophylakion at the east end of the building.

The Justinianic Hagia Sophia

After the ruthless suppression of his political opponents in the Nikē uprising, the emperor Justinian celebrated his newly consolidated position by rebuilding a far more splendid cathedral than that which his enemies had destroyed. Calling on a mathematician and a physicist, Anthemius of Tralles and Isidore of Miletus, he marshaled all the resources of the empire in the construction of the most daring and most original monument Byzantine architecture would ever produce. In five short years (532–37) the old basilica of Theodosius was replaced with a light and lofty domed structure whose fabric still stands substantially intact today.

Justinian's Hagia Sophia does not easily lend itself to summary treatment. In sheer size it is one of the largest man-made structures in the world; its great vaulted nave easily surpasses all the vaulted interiors of antiquity and the Middle Ages for space enclosed within a single clear span. In engineering it is as puzzling today as it was terrifying to Procopius, to whom it appeared to soar aloft without reliable support, threatening the safety of those within. Religiously and historically the importance of the monument is impossible to calculate. As cathedral it was the center of Constantinople's religious life, and as patriarchal seat it was the heart of Eastern Christendom for nearly a millennium. Every pilgrim hoped to be able to tell of visiting it, and every Byzantine prince hoped to build his own local replica of it, whether in Kiev or in Benevento. Sheathed in marble and gold, its splendor the medieval mind translated into legend, and far beyond the orbit of Byzantium the abbot Suger of St. Denis was most delighted when he found travelers who would assure him that his new church was a match for Hagia Sophia. The encomiums of poets, the praise of historians, the hard analyses of archaeologists—these comprise a vast literature on the church, but somehow the building seems never to be adequately described, and the more that is written the more problems emerge in its discussion.

Limiting oneself to the modern bibliography on the church, the two most significant turning points in the recent history of Hagia Sophia are 1847 and 1934. In May of 1847 the Swiss architects Gaspard and Giuseppe Fossati, at the invitation of the Sultan Abdülmecit I, began a major two-year project of restoration, and for the first time since its conversion to a mosque in 1453 the building was accessible for a while to Western scholars. Erecting scaffolding throughout the mosque, the Fossatis concentrated on consolidating the dome and vaults, straightening columns, cleaning and again covering up the mosaics, and then plastering and painting both inside and out. Though their published scholarly contribution was slight—a volume of lithographs and a slender description of the restoration work—their project gave strong impetus to other studies. Salzenberg took advantage of the opportunity of working with them to publish in folio the first measured plans and sections, which became the point of departure for archaeological discussion of the building for nearly a century. The work of Lethaby and Swainson, and Antoniades' monumental three-volume study, enlarged on Salzenberg's work by describing the building and its history, part by part and period by period; for completeness their works have hardly been rivaled to this day.

Another epoch was inaugurated in 1934, for in November of that year the Ministry of Education, acting on the proposal of Atatürk, converted the mosque of Ayasofya into a museum. The end of religious services in the building marked the beginning of the cleaning and systematic structural study of the monument, a work which is not yet complete. The largest single problem area under study has been the statics of the vaulting—the engineering of the 32-meter ribbed dome and its complex system of supports in half-domes to the east and west and massive piers to the north and south. It was commonly known from historical sources that considerable damage had been done to Justinian's church by the earthquakes that Constantinople has experienced. Even within Justinian's lifetime, barely twenty years after the dedication of the church, the earthquake of 557 so severely weakened the structure that the following year the whole dome fell, and it took another five years to rebuild. The new dome was steeper than the first and lighted with a ring of 42 windows at the base. Another quake in 989 brought down the western segment of the dome, and a third in 1346 brought down the eastern segment and with it the great eastern arch. The problem of distinguishing one revision from another in this long building history and of reconstructing the original design of Anthemius and Isidore can be resolved only with painstaking measurement and observation of the existing fabric. This is the task that Conant, Emerson, Van Nice, and Mainstone set for themselves in a series of individual articles; on a more comprehensive scale, this is the task that Van Nice has undertaken in his monumental architectural survey. A folio of Van Nice's plates has appeared—possibly the most detailed rendering ever accorded a monument of this scale—and it will be supplemented eventually with a text volume of description and analysis.

Since the secularization of Hagia Sophia the Byzantine Institute of the United States and the Dumbarton Oaks Field Committee, which sponsored Van Nice's research, have also gradually cleaned and restored all the mosaic decoration of the building. This work, carried forward by Underwood, Whittemore, Hawkins, and Mango, was published by them in a series of separate studies. Meanwhile less ambitious investigations have been carried out on many different parts or details of the structure which, taken together, help to fill out our picture of the whole building.

Outside the church the German Archaeological Institute, under Schneider's direction, excavated the area west of the church where, in addition to the propylaeum of the Theodosian basilica, they uncovered the foundations of Justinian's atrium. The atrium, wider than long, consisted of a portico which alternated a pier with two columns on three sides, as Schneider reconstructed it. At about the same time Swift studied the buttresses which were added outside Hagia Sophia at various periods, though his dating is not always reliable. Emerson and Van Nice examined the stair turrets of the west façade, in the southern one of which they found the foundations of the first minaret erected on the mosque. More recently Dirimtekin, the director of the Ayasofya Museum, took the opportunity afforded by repair work to study the baptistery as well as the structures at the southwest corner of the building, which he identified as the patriarchate. The latter study is complemented by Janin's research on the patriarchate. A new study of the atrium and nartheces by Strube has proposed that the outer narthex was originally open and was not enclosed with doors and windows until the second Justinianic dedication of the church.

Within the church proper no real excavation has ever been conducted. Ramazanoğlu, the earlier director of the Ayasofya Museum, began soundings under the pavement of the nave, but the work was not carried very far, and a not very informative note by Mamboury was the only report published. The cleaning and repair of other parts of the church, however, has contributed to the resolution of some problems. The Istituto Centrale di Restauro of Rome was invited to clean and study the great brass doors and other brass fixings in the church, and this has resolved earlier speculation on the origin of these elements. Hawkins' study of the plaster decoration was able to distinguish the original elements from their later substitutes or imitations. Similarly Sheppard has tried to distinguish sixth from ninth century carved wooden tie beams by radio-carbon dating. Finally, working from literary sources as well as from the markings in the pavement, Mamboury, Xydis, and I have tried to piece together the evidence for the liturgical furnishings and the liturgical divisions of the church—findings which should be compared with the earlier conclusions reached by Antoniades and Ebersolt.

As some of the structural problems of Hagia Sophia gradually find solution, the larger questions of its place in architectural history begin to clarify themselves. Regarding the sources that lie behind the architecture, the pendulum of opinion has swung radically from the East to Rome and has come to rest somewhere between, in the building traditions of the Late Roman Empire as current in the Aegean area. At the turn of the century Strygowski, looking at formal resemblances rather than building techniques, could call Hagia Sophia "purely Armenian" in conception. Rivoira and Zaloziecky, on the other hand, pointed out the continuity in building traditions between Hagia Sophia and the architecture of Rome. But, to be more accurate, the Roman traditions involved are not those of Italy but those of the great Hellenistic cities of Asia Minor where Deichmann and Ward Perkins have traced the history of the stone-bonded concrete walls and light brick vaults that characterize the masonry of Hagia Sophia.

Nevertheless, while accepting this account of the building techniques in use at Hagia Sophia, Krautheimer points out that the structure and design need not have the same origin. For the double-shell design of the church—that is, the central space surrounded by ambulatory spaces—and for the complex interplay of spaces through diagonal niches Krautheimer suggests sources in Early Christian tetraconch churches and palace octagons. Grabar, on the other hand, would insist on the dominance of centrally planned martyria in the East.

Scholarship on Hagia Sophia, in spite of the long strides taken in recent decades, is still a long way from any comprehensive or synthetic treatment of the monument. Since 1934 only Swift has attempted such a work, and in view of the important archaeological work under way at the time, it must be said that his effort was premature. Other general discussions of the building by Schneider, Jantzen, Kähler, or Sanpaolesi provide the reader only with well-informed introductions to the building. Kähler's work stands out, however, for its systematic photographic coverage of the church. Intended for popularization are the official guide books of the Ayasofya Museum by Gülekli and Dirimtekin, which include an introduction to the history of the monument in Turkish times.

Bibliography

The Old Hagia Sophia

A.M. Schneider, "Die vorjustinianische Sophienkirche," *BZ* 36 (1936), 77–85.

A.M. Schneider, *Die Grabung im Westhof der Sophienkirche zu Istanbul*, Istanbuler Forschungen 8 (Berlin, 1936).

G. Millet, "Sainte-Sophie avant Justinien," *Orientalia christiana periodica* 13 (1947), 597–612.

F. Dirimtekin, "Le skeuophylakion de sainte-Sophie," *REB* 19 (1961), 397–400.

Mathews, *The Early Churches of Constantinople*, pp. 11–19.

The Justinianic Hagia Sophia

Important studies prior to 1934

Gaspard Fossati, *Aya Sofia, Constantinople, As Recently Restored by Order of H.M. the Sultan Abdul Mediid* (London, 1852).

W. Salzenburg, *Altchristliche Baudenkmale von Constantinopel vom V bis XII Jahrhundert* (Berlin, 1854).

Giuseppe Fossati, *Rilievi storico-artistici sulla architettura bizantina dal IV al XV secolo, notizie intorno alle scoperte fatte in Santa Sofia a Constantinopoli, Maggio 1847–Luglio 1849* (Milan, 1890).

W.R. Lethaby and H. Swainson, *The Church of Sancta Sophia, Constantinople* (London, 1894).

E. Antoniades, *Ekphrasis tēs Hagias Sophias*, 3 vols. (Athens, 1907–9).

J. Ebersolt, *Sainte-Sophie de Constantinople, étude de topographie d'après les cérémonies* (Paris, 1910).

C. Gurlitt, *Die Baukunst Konstantinopels* (Berlin, 1912), pp. 20–22.

Studies of statics and structure

K.J. Conant, "The First Dome of St. Sophia and Its Rebuilding," *AJA* 43 (1939), 589–91.

W. Emerson and R.L. Van Nice, "Hagia Sophia: Preliminary Report of a Recent Examination of the Structure," *AJA* 47 (1943), 403–36.

W. Emerson and R.L. Van Nice, "Hagia Sophia: The Collapse of the First Dome," *Archaeology* 4 (1951), 94–103.

W. Emerson and R.L. Van Nice, "Hagia Sophia: The Construction of the Second Dome and Its Later Repairs," *Archaeology* 4 (1951), 162–71.

R.L. Van Nice, "The Structure of St. Sophia," *Architectural Forum* 118 (1963), 131–39.

R.L. Van Nice, "St. Sophia's Structure: A New Assessment of the Half Domes," *Architectural Forum* 119 (1964), 45–49.

R.L. Van Nice, *Saint Sophia in Istanbul: An Architectural Survey* (Washington, 1965).

R.J. Mainstone, "The Structure of the Church of St. Sophia, Istanbul," *Transactions of the Newcomen Society* 38 (1965–66), 23–49.

R.J. Mainstone, "Justinian's Church of St. Sophia, Istanbul: Recent Studies of Its Construction and First Partial Reconstruction," *Architectural History* 12 (1969), 39–49.

R.J. Mainstone, "The Reconstruction of the Tympana of St. Sophia at Istanbul," *DOP* 23–24 (1969–70), 355–68.

The mosaics

T. Whittemore, *The Mosaics of St. Sophia at Istanbul. Preliminary Reports* (Oxford, 1933, 1936, 1942, 1952).

P.A. Underwood, "Notes on the Work of the Byzantine Institute in Istanbul: 1954," *DOP* 9-10 (1956), 291-94.

P.A. Underwood and E.J.W. Hawkins, "The Portrait of the Emperor Alexander," *DOP* 15 (1961), 187-217.

C. Mango, *Materials for the Study of the Mosaics of St. Sophia at Istanbul*, Dumbarton Oaks Studies 8 (Washington, D.C., 1962).

C. Mango and E.J.W. Hawkins, "The Apse Mosaics of St. Sophia at Istanbul," *DOP* 19 (1965), 3-51.

Particular studies

E.H. Swift, "The Latins at Hagia Sophia," *AJA* 39 (1935), 458-74.

E. Mamboury, "Topographie de sainte-Sophie, le sanctuaire et la solea, le mitatorion, etc.," *Atti del V Congresso di studi bizantini* 2. *Studi bizantini e neoellenici*, 6 (Rome, 1940), 203.

A.M. Schneider, *Die Grabung in Westhof der Sophienkirche zu Istanbul*, Istanbuler Forschungen 12 (Berlin, 1941).

S.G. Xydis, "The Chancel Barrier, Solea, and Ambo of Hagia Sophia," *AB* 29 (1947), 1-24.

W. Emerson and R.L. Van Nice, "Hagia Sophia and the First Minaret Erected after the Conquest of Constantinople," *AJA* 54 (1950), 33-40.

E. Mamboury, "1945: Les sondages à l'intérieur de Ste. Sophie," *Byzantion* 21 (1951), 437-38.

L. Borrelli Vlad, "Attività dell' istituto all' estero: Turchia," *Bolletino dell' istituto centrale del restauro* 31-32 (1957), 182-87.

C. Bertelli, "Notizia preliminare sul restauro di alcune porte di S. Sofia à Istanbul," *Bolletino dell' istituto centrale del restauro* 34-35 (1958), 58-115.

R. Janin, "Le palais patriarchal de Constantinople byzantine," *REB* 20 (1962), 131-55.

F. Dirimtekin, "Ayasofya Baptisteri: The Baptistery of Saint Sophia," *Türk Arkeoloji Dergisi* 12, 2 (1963), 54-87.

F. Dirimtekin, "Le local du patriarcat à Sainte Sophie," *IM* 13-14 (1963-64), 113-27.

E. Hawkins, "Plaster and Stucco Cornices in Hagia Sophia, Istanbul," *Congrès internationale des études byzantines* 12 (Belgrade, 1964), 3, 131-35.

D. Sheppard, "A Radiocarbon Date for the Wooden Tie Beams in the West Gallery of St. Sophia, Istanbul," *DOP* 19 (1965), 237-40.

Mathews, *The Early Churches of Constantinople*, pp. 88-99.

C. Strube, *Die westliche Eingangsseite der Kirchen von Konstantinopel in justinianischer Zeit* (Weisbaden, 1973), pp. 13-105.

Studies of the sources of Hagia Sophia

J. Strzygowski, *Origins of Christian Church Art*, trans. O.M. Dalton (Oxford, 1923).

G.T. Rivoira, *L'architettura romana* (Milan, 1921).

G.A. Andreades, "Die Sophienkathedrale von Konstantinopel," *Kunstwissenschaftliche Forschungen* 1 (1931), 33–94.

H. Sedlmayr, "Zur Geschichte des justinianischen Architektursystems," *BZ* 35 (1935), 38–69.

W.R. Zaloziecky, *Die Sophienkirke in Konstantinopel und ihre Stellung in der Geschichte der abendländischen Architektur:* Studi di antichità cristiana 12 (Vatican City, 1936).

A. Grabar, *Martyrium: Recherches sur le culte des reliques et l'art chrétien antique*, 2 vols. (Paris, 1943–46).

J.B. Ward Perkins, "The Italian Element in Late Roman and Early Medieval Architecture," *Proceedings of the British Academy* 32 (1947), 1–41.

F.W. Deichmann, *Studien zur Architektur Konstantinopels* (Baden-Baden, 1956).

J.B. Ward Perkins, "Building Methods of Early Byzantine Architecture," in D. Talbot Rice, *The Great Palace of the Byzantine Emperors, Second Report* (Edinburgh, 1958), pp. 52–104.

Krautheimer, *Early Christian and Byzantine Architecture*, pp. 153–70.

General studies since 1934

A.M. Schneider, *Die Hagia Sophia zu Konstantinopel* (Berlin, 1939).

E.H. Swift, *Hagia Sophia* (New York, 1940).

N.C. Gülekli, *Hagia Sophia* (Istanbul, n.d.).

F. Dirimtekin, *Saint Sophia Museum* (Istanbul, n.d.).

P. Sanpaolesi, *Santa Sofia à Costantinopoli* (Florence, 1965).

H. Jantzen, *Die Hagia Sophia des Kaisers Justinian in Konstantinopel* (Cologne, 1967).

H. Kähler and C. Mango, *Hagia Sophia*, trans. E. Childs (London, 1967).

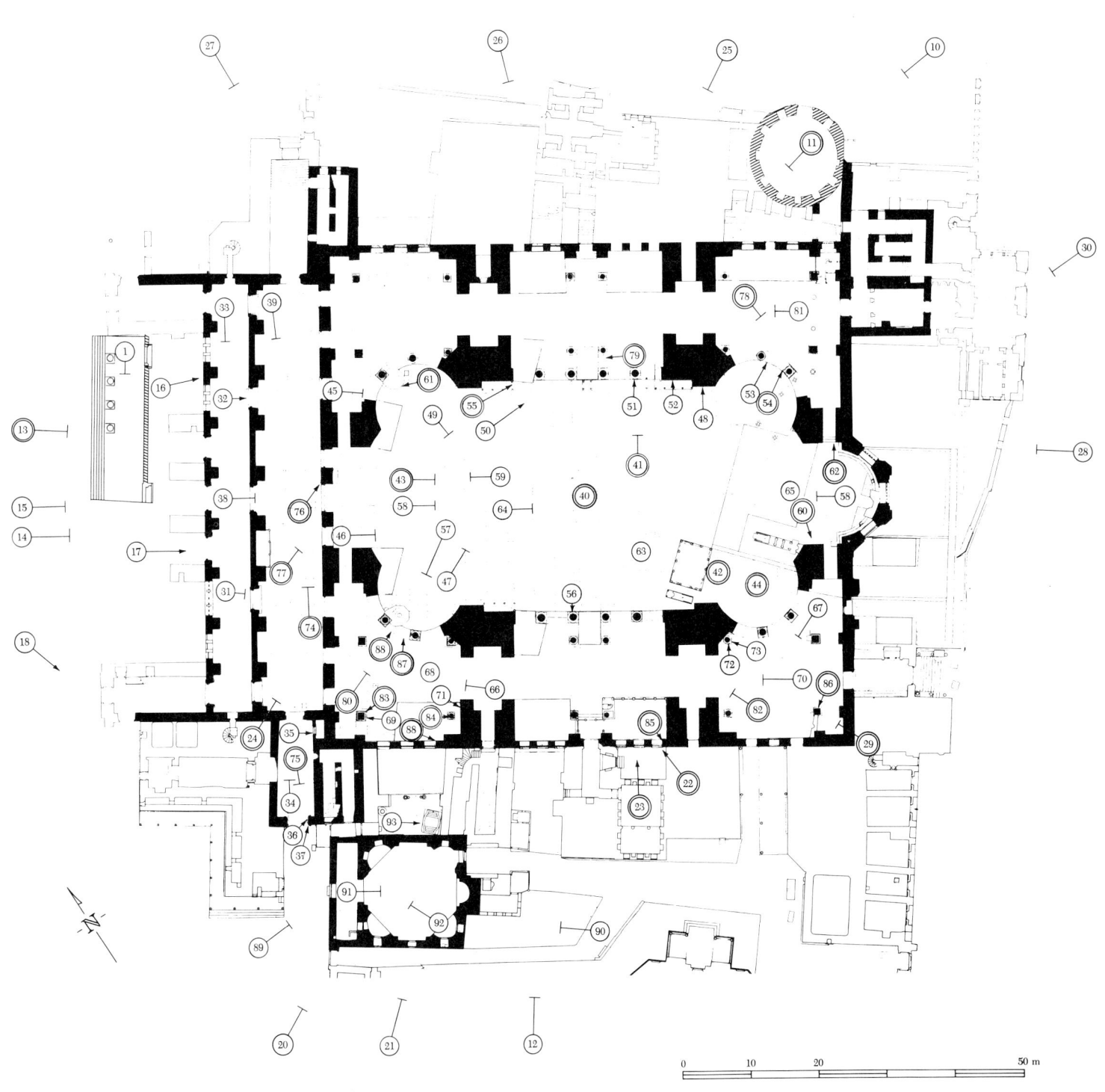

from Van Nice

Hagia Sophia 269

31-1

31-2

31-3

31-1 The propylaeum excavation in 1936, viewed from the north. Photo Schneider, German Archaeological Institute, Istanbul, 1033
31-2 Frieze of lambs from the propylaeum, detail. M19000
31-3 Frieze of lambs from the propylaeum. M18815

31-4

31-5

31-6

31-7

31-4 Pediment cornice from the propylaeum. M4866
31-5 Detail of the architrave from the propylaeum. M18820
31-6 Pilaster capital from the propylaeum. M19003
31-7 Capital from the propylaeum. M18907

31-8

31-9

31-8 Coffering from the propylaeum. M18905
31-9 Tongue and dart molding from the propylaeum. M18915
31-10 The skeuophylakion from the northeast. M18302
31-11 The skeuophylakion: blocked windows on the upper level, viewed from the northeast. M26705

31-10

31-11

31-12

276 Hagia Sophia

31-13

31-12 General view from the south. Photo Josephine Powell, T 4–1
31-13 The dome and western half-dome from the west. M4523

31-14

31-15

31-14 The west façade, 1847–1849, from a drawing by Gaspard Fossati in the author's collection. Photo Josephine Powell, 1764–5
31-15 The west façade. M18106

31-16

31-17

31-18

31-19

31-16 Detail of 31–15, north bays. M19007
31-17 The right-hand portal in the west façade. M4816
31-18 Remains of the south colonnade of the atrium, 1873, from a drawing by Mary Walker. The Van Millingen collection, Burrows Library of Byzantine and Modern Greek, King's College, University of London
31-19 A capital from the atrium colonnade, 1873, from a drawing by Mary Walker. The Van Millingen collection, Burrows Library of Byzantine and Modern Greek, King's College, University of London

31-20

31-21

280   Hagia Sophia

31-22

31-23

31-20 General view from the southwest, 1886, Kondakov, *Vizantitskiia Tserkvi*, plate 1
31-21 The south flank from the southwest. M8829
31-22 The south tympanum from the southeast. M25339
31-23 Gallery window on the south flank. M337

31-24

31-24 Western half-dome and adjacent vaulting from above, from the southwest minaret. M12124A
31-25 General view from the northeast with the skeuophylakion in the left foreground. M25613
31-26 The north tympanum and the dome. M17130
31-27 The northwest corner of the building. M3610

31-25

31-26

31-27

Hagia Sophia   283

31-28

31-28 General view of the east end, 1909. Photo Sir I. Benjamin Stone collection, The Birmingham Public Libraries
31-29 The dome from the southeast minaret. M12705A
31-30 The east end from the northeast. M408

31-29

31-30

31-31 A view from the outer narthex to the inner narthex. M6413A

31-32

31-33

31-34

31-35

31-32 Second door from the north in the outer narthex. Photo Marburg, 2790
31-33 The outer narthex from the north. M6430A
31-34 The southwest vestibule from the south. M24703
31-35 Detail of the plaster molding in the southwest vestibule. Photo Dumbarton Oaks Field Committee, H60.233

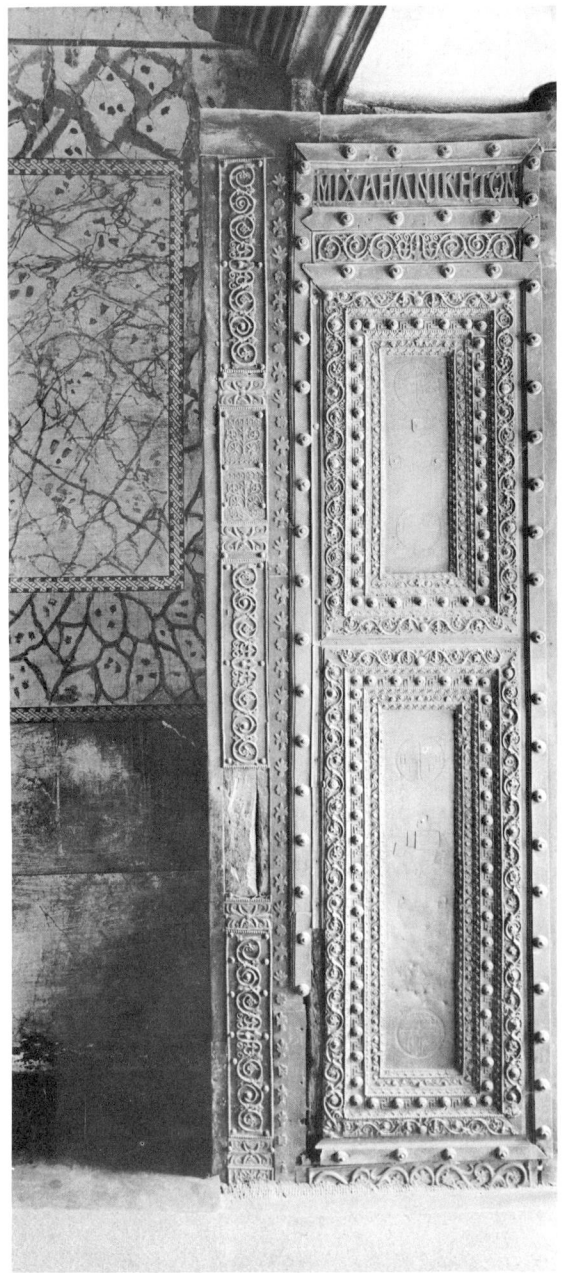

31-36

31-37

31-38

31-39

31-36 The bronze door in the southwest vestibule, before its removal. Photo Marburg, 2771
31-37 Detail of the bronze door in the southwest vestibule, before its removal. Photo Marburg, 2778
31-38 The main portal into the nave. M6416A
31-39 The inner narthex from the north. M10710

31-40

31-41

31-40 The main dome, with the west below. Photo Josephine Powell, T 4–16
31-41 The northeast quadrant of the dome. M25323

31-42

31-43

31-42 The vaulting of the dome, half-dome, and southeast niche. M10736A
31-43 General view of the nave and its vaulting from the west. M27804
31-44 The southeast niche. M4120
31-45 The view into the nave from the northwest niche. M27719

31-44

31-45

31-46

31-46 General view of the nave from the west. M24809A
31-47 The north wall of the nave. M4133

294   Hagia Sophia

31-47

31-48 Detail of the revetment on the northeast pier of the nave. M16154
31-49 The south colonnade on the ground floor. M13213
31-50 Detail of the capitals of the north arcade on the ground level, from the west. M16207
31-51 The easternmost capital from the north colonnade, ground level. M16215
31-52 Detail of the lower cornice on the northeast pier. M16160

31-48

31-49

296   Hagia Sophia

31-50

31-51

31-52

31-53

31-54

31-55

31-56

31-53 Detail of the revetment in an arch of the northeast niche, ground level. M16035
31-54 Detail of the revetment in the arches of the northeast niche, gallery level. M16049
31-55 Detail of the capitals of the north arcade on the gallery level, from the west. M16223
31-56 A column base in the south arcade, ground level. M4127
31-57 The southwest niche from the northeast. M13030

31-57

Hagia Sophia

31-58

31-59

31-60

31-61

31-58 General view of the nave from the east. Photo Dumbarton Oaks Field Committee, H59.9
31-59 The west wall of the nave. Photo Dumbarton Oaks Field Committee, SIIIA1.1 (59)
31-60 The revetment on the south wall of the sanctuary, gallery level. M13023
31-61 The northwest niche, gallery level. M13319

Hagia Sophia   301

31-62 Detail of the revetment on the north wall of the sanctuary, gallery level. M25018
31-63 The porphyry disc in the nave. M25329
31-64 The pavement of the nave, from the west. M25170
31-65 Polychrome pavement in the sanctuary. Photo Dumbarton Oaks Field Committee, 116.1939

31-62

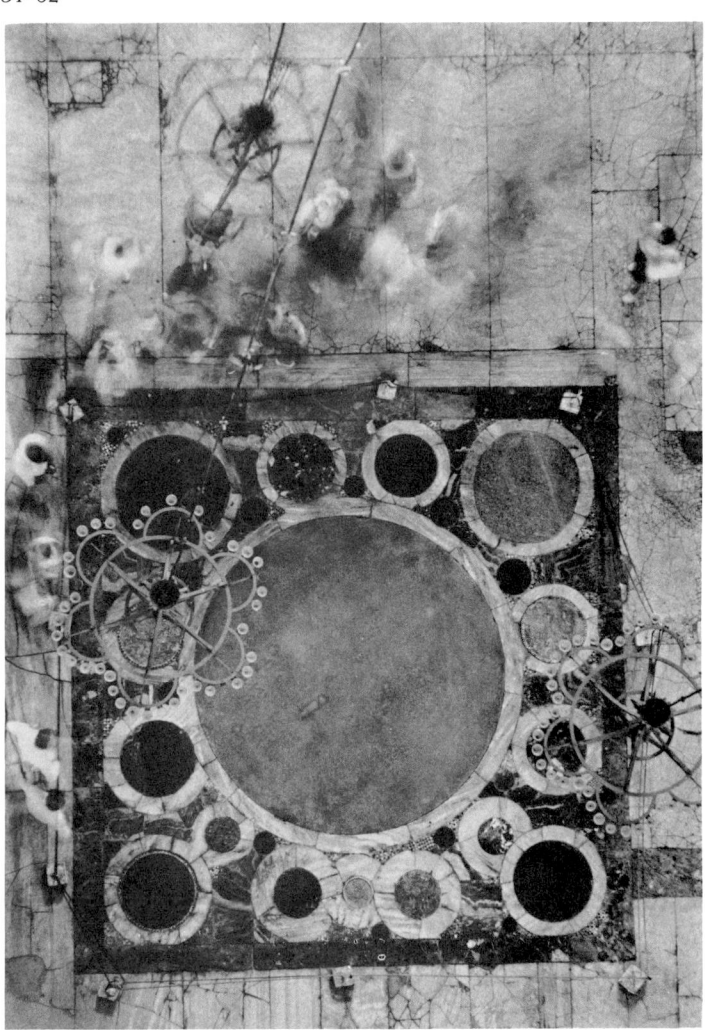

31-63

302   Hagia Sophia

31-64

31-65

Hagia Sophia 303

31-66

31-67

31-68

304   Hagia Sophia

31-69

31-66 The west bay of the south aisle, viewed from the east. M10822
31-67 The east bay of the south aisle, viewed from the northeast. M4657
31-68 The vaulting of the west bay of the south aisle. M10824
31-69 A pier capital in the west bay of the south aisle. M1010

31-70

31-71

31-72

31-73

306   Hagia Sophia

31-74

31-75

31-70   The south aisle from the east. M4651
31-71   A detail of the cornice in the west bay of the south aisle. M5010
31-72   A capital in the east bay of the south aisle. M16130
31-73   A different view of 31-72. M16112
31-74   The west gallery from the south. M25058
31-75   The room over the southwest vestibule from the north. Photo Dumbarton Oaks Field Committee, H.66.145

Hagia Sophia   307

31-76

31-76	Capital and wooden tie-beam in the west gallery arcade. M13226
31-77	The arcade of the west gallery from the southwest. M6312
31-78	The east bay of the north gallery, viewed from the north. M6335
31-79	The colonnade of the north gallery from the east. M6506
31-80	The west bay of the south gallery from the south. M27921
31-81	The north gallery from the east. M13004
31-82	The south gallery from the southeast. M13132

31-77

31-78

31-79

31-80

31-81

31-82

Hagia Sophia   309

31-83

31-84

31-85

31-86

31-83 A capital in the south gallery. M24919
31-84 A capital in the south gallery. M24925
31-85 A detail of the window frame in the central bay of the south aisle. M24903
31-86 A capital in the south gallery. M4742
31-87 Parapet slab in the west bay of the south gallery. M24951
31-88 Parapet slab in the west bay of the south gallery. M24969
31-89 The baptistry from the southwest. Photo Dumbarton Oaks Field Committee, SIIE1.1 (36)
31-90 The baptistry from the southeast. M22721

31-87

31-88

31-89

31-90

Hagia Sophia   311

31-91

31-92

31-93

31-91 The interior of the baptistry from the west. M7110
31-92 The interior of the baptistry from the southeast. M7115
31-93 The baptismal font, north of the baptistry. Photo Artamonoff, Dumbarton Oaks Field Committee, RA462a

32

Şeyh Murat Mescidi

Located at the northeast corner of the present Kopça Sok. and Altı Pağa Sok., not far from the Pantepoptēs church, the Şeyh Murat Mescidi was already in ruins in Paspates' time and has since perished, apparently without ever being photographed. Paspates published a drawing of the south flank and left us the only informative description of the church, remarking on its cross-domed plan, its overall dimensions of roughly 15 by 13 meters, and its construction in bands of brick and cut stone. Earlier von Warsberg had mentioned a narthex with three domes; and a little later Mary Walker's sketch of the north window seems to show the recessed brick masonry of the Comnenian period. By the time Grosvenor observed the church in 1895 it had been replaced with a dervish tekke, and when Mamboury inspected the site after the 1917 fire in that section only a few sculptured fragments remained. Modern houses have since replaced the ruins.

Bibliography

A.F. von Warsberg, *Ein Sommer im Orient* (Vienna, 1869), p. 236.

A.G. Paspates, *Byzantinai meletai,* pp. 382–83.

C. Curtis and M. Walker, *Broken Bits of Byzantium* (London, 1890), fig. 52–56.

E.A. Grosvenor, *Constantinople* (Boston, 1895), vol. 12, p. 470.

E. Mamboury, *Constantinople, Tourists' Guide* (Constantinople, 1925), pp. 229–30.

32-1

32-2

32-1 View from the south in Paspates' lithograph, 1877
32-2 Detail of the north window from Walker's sketch, 1890

33

Şeyh Süleyman Mescidi

Byzantine archaeologists have paid scant attention to this monument, and the few comments that have been made offer widely divergent interpretations of the original function of the building. Grosvenor and other early authors suggested that it served as a library to the nearby Pantokratōr monastery. There is, however, no supporting archaeological evidence; the building is a full 250 meters distant from the Pantokratōr, and its masonry is not Comnenian but Early Byzantine. Eyice's notion that the Şeyh Süleyman was a funerary chapel, a proposal he made on the basis of explorations by Fıratlı, is equally insecure. The substructure of the building, consisting of a segmented octagonal vault surrounded by eight deep niches, could conceivably have been used for burial, but no evidence of burial has been found on the site.

A third hypothesis, that advanced by Ebersolt, is the most convincing, for Fıratlı's study turned up positive evidence that the building might have been used as a baptistery. Fıratlı noted a six-column cistern of Early Byzantine date 6 or 8 meters to the north, and aligned on the same axis with this building; it had water pipes leading in the direction of the Şeyh Süleyman. The plan of the Şeyh Süleyman lends support to the baptistery hypothesis, for, apart from the absence of a narthex, it duplicates the plan of the only securely identified baptistery in Constantinople—that of Hagia Sophia. Octagonal at the upper level, it expands through corner niches at ground level into a square plan.

In Turkish times the building appears to have suffered several revisions, especially in the doors and windows. Made into a mosque in the sixteenth century under Mehmet the Conqueror, it was restored, according to Eyice, under Mustafa III in the eighteenth century. The dome might have been remade at that time, but the elliptical arches under it appear to be of original Byzantine construction.

Bibliography

E.A. Grosvenor, *Constantinople* (Boston, 1900), vol. 2, pp. 427–28.

J. Ebersolt, *Rapport sommaire sur un mission à Constantinople* (Paris, 1911), pp. 13–14.

C. Gurlitt, *Die Baukunst Konstantinopels* (Berlin, 1912), pp. 92–93.

N. Fıratlı, "Some Unknown Byzantine Cisterns of Istanbul," *Bulletin officiel du touring et automobile club de Turquie*, 120 (Jan. 1952), 3–6.

S. Eyice, *Istanbul, Petit guide à travers les monuments byzantines et turcs* (Istanbul, 1955), p. 59.

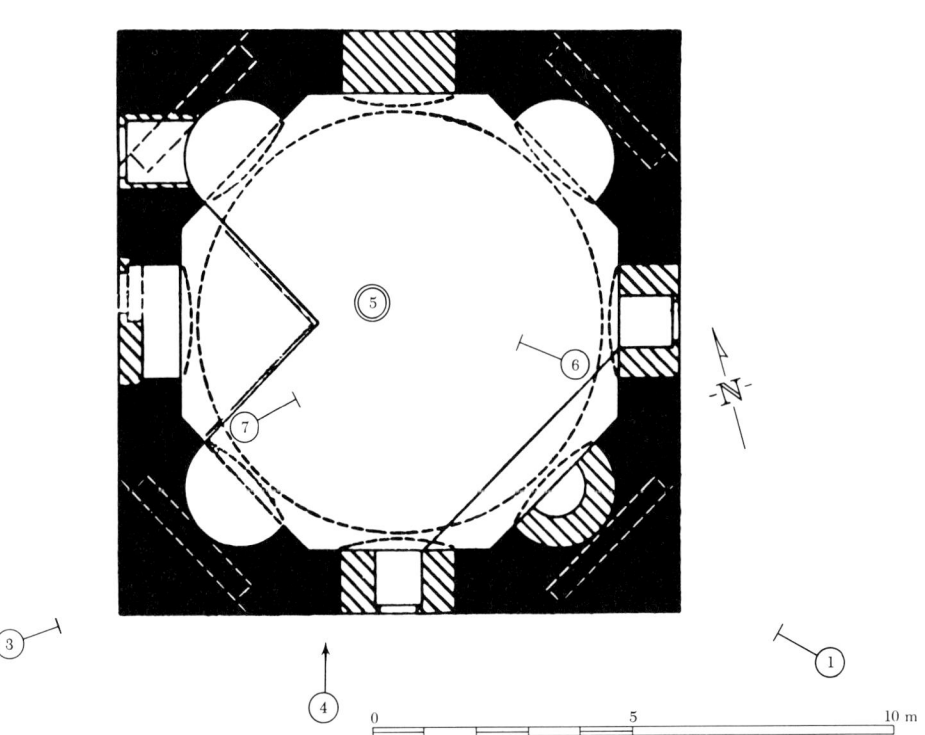

from Gurlitt

33-1

33-2

316 Şeyh Süleyman Mescidi

33-3

33-1 View from the southeast. M11835
33-2 View from the northwest. M22353
33-3 General view from the west. M11822

33-4

33-5

33-6

33-7

33-4 Detail of the masonry on the south side of the building. M17636
33-5 The vaulting of the dome, with the west below. M22325
33-6 Interior view from the southeast. M22333
33-7 Interior view from the southwest. M22337

Şeyh Süleyman Mescidi

34

Theotokos tōn Chalkoprateiōn (The Mother-of-God of the Bronze-workers' District), and Hag. Iakōbos (St. James). Acem Ağa Mescidi.

The Chalkoprateia church, a neighbor of Hagia Sophia, ranked as Constantinople's most important shrine to the Mother of God, whose cincture it housed. The history of the shrine and the cult of relics associated with it are treated in accounts by Jugie, Ebersolt, and Janin. Unfortunately the archaeology of the site has not been as thoroughly studied.

Since the abandonment early in the twentieth century of the Acem Ağa Mescidi, which had occupied the apse of the church since 1755, the site has gradually deteriorated. Mamboury in 1912 was the first to identify the building's remains, but beyond a superficial description he made no report of his finds. In 1924, Lathoud and Pezaud published photographs and a summary plan of the site. They remarked on the extraordinary dimensions of the building which make it the largest basilica discovered so far in Constantinople, and they placed its foundation date between 450 and 460, seeking to reconcile the different accounts of its founding in Byzantine sources.

More recently Kleiss has made a survey of the Chalkoprateia, uncovering the cruciform crypt in the sanctuary and reporting the substructures of an octagonal building tangent to the north wall of the atrium. The latter he identified as a baptistery, but in so doing he neglected the evidence of the fourteenth century frescoes photographed by Mango in 1953. The frescoes, which have since disappeared, depicted scenes of the Infancy and of the death of Zacharias. In the chronicles of medieval travelers, relics of St. Zacharias and of Christ's infancy are mentioned in connection with the chapel of Hag. Iakōbos, located in the atrium of the Chalkoprateia; the octagon, then, must certainly be identified with that chapel and therefore be recognized as one of a very small number of firmly established martyria in Constantinople.

The plan of the Chalkoprateia very strongly resembled that of the Stoudios basilica. An atrium lay before the church; there were galleries above the aisles on either side, a synthronon in the apse, and a crypt beneath the altar. Under Basil I (867–86) the church was rebuilt and a dome was added over the nave.

Bibliography

M. Jugie, "L'église des Chalcopratia et le culte de la ceinture de la Sainte Vierge à Constantinople," *EO* 16 (1913), 308–312.

D. Lathoud and P. Pezaud, "Le Sanctuaire de la Vierge aux Chalcopratia," *EO* 23 (1924), 36–62.

E. Mamboury, *Constantinople, Tourists' Guide* (Constantinople, 1925), pp. 230–31.

J. Ebersolt, *Constantinople, recueille d'études d'archéologie et d'histoire: Les anciens sanctuaires de Constantinople* (Paris, 1951), pp. 54–60.

W. Kleiss, "Neue Befunde zur Chalkopratenkirche in Istanbul," *IM* 15 (1965), 149–67; "Grabungen im Bereich der Chalkopratenkirche in Istanbul, 1965," *IM* 16 (1966), 217–40.

Janin, *La géographie*, pp. 237–42, 253–55.

C. Mango, "Notes on Byzantine Monuments: Frescoes in the Octagon of St. Mary Chalkoprateia," *DOP* 23–24 (1969–70), 369–72.

Mathews, *The Early Churches of Constantinople*, pp. 28–33.

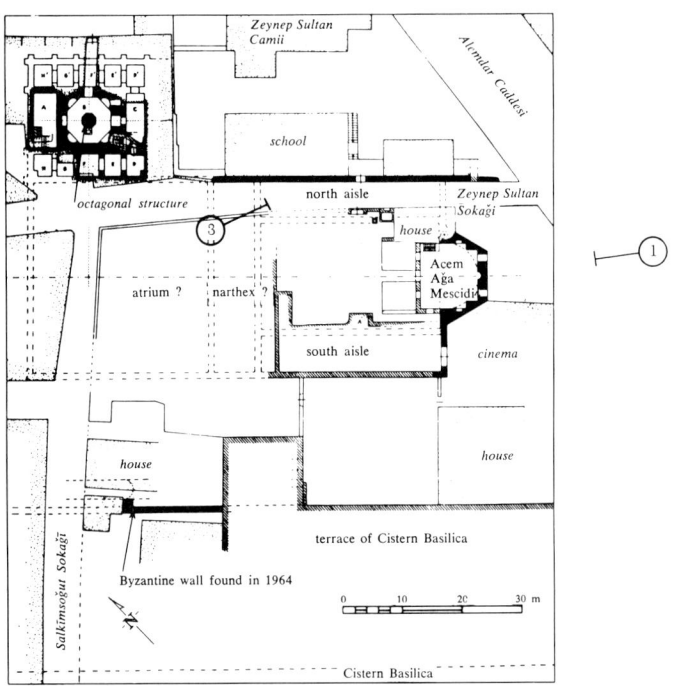

from Kleiss

34-1

34-2

34-3

34-1 General view from above, from the east. M12631
34-2 Capital from the church, now in the Istanbul Archaeological Museum. M16366
34-3 Remains of the north wall, viewed from the southwest. M4106

Theotokos tōn Chalkoprateiōn 321

35

Theotokos tou Libos (The Mother-of-God of Lips), and Hag. Iōannēs Prodromos tou Libos (St. John the Forerunner of Lips). Fenarı Isa Camii.

This church of Theotokos was erected by Constantine Lips, an officer under Leo VI, in 907; a second church, dedicated to the Baptist, was added alongside it to the south at the close of the thirteenth century by Theodora, the widow of Michael VIII Palaeologus. As the earliest dated Macedonian foundation in Constantinople, the north church is a key monument in the history of Byzantine architecture and has been one of the most thoroughly studied monuments of the city. The excavation reports carry a fuller photographic documentation than that available for any other church in the city except Hagia Sophia.

Except for the addition of a minaret at the southwest corner, the conversion of this double church to a mosque in the late fifteenth century did not involve any substantial changes in the structure. A disastrous fire in 1633, however, and the subsequent restoration in 1636 modified the building considerably. The columns were removed from the naves of both churches and replaced with broad pointed arches, the walls were scraped of their decoration and plastered, both domes were reconstructed, and the fenestration was revised throughout. It was in this condition when Ebersolt and Van Millingen prepared their reports on the building. In spite of the transformations the churches had undergone, they recognized the basic elements of the plan—a quincunx or cross-in-square in the north church and an ambulatory-type plan in the south, with an outer aisle or narthex running around the west and south of the whole complex.

In 1917 another fire swept the building and left it not only in ruins but deserted as well, since this entire quarter of the city was destroyed in the conflagration. Brunov studied the ruins in 1924, and his reconstruction of the north church has been the starting point for most subsequent writing about the building. To Brunov the church represented a "five-aisled" type of plan—that is, a cross-in-square plan with outer flanking aisles to the north and south and five apses to the east. Brunov pointed out that the prothesis of the south church was originally an outer south chapel of the north church, in bond with it and of the same masonry. To the north, he proposed, there would have been a symmetrical development. On the roof level are found four diminutive domed chapels, one at each corner of the plan; those at the west were connected by a gallery over the narthex (since destroyed), but those at the east could not have been reached, according to Brunov, unless one reconstructed outer flanking aisles running the length of the church with galleries above them.

This five-aisled reconstruction enjoyed wide circulation and the excavation of the site by Macridy in 1929 (report not published until 1964) seemed to confirm the hypothesis. The foundations of the fifth apse were found at the northeast corner of the building. Macridy also believed he found evidence of an earlier church beneath the tenth century building, and he discovered beneath the Turkish pavement a wealth of fragments of the decoration of the church. Macridy's interpretation of evidence, however, has been contradicted in some points by the more recent excavations of Megaw. In 1960 the Ministry of Mosques began the restoration of the structure by replacing the vaulting of the outer narthex. The work of restoration was continued by the Byzantine Institute under Megaw, who initiated new limited excavations to test Macridy's findings in the north church. Megaw found no evidence of an outer north aisle except for the little apsed chapel at the northeast corner, contradicting the Brunov five-aisled hypothesis. He found no evidence, either, of an earlier structure on the site. He proposed a reconstruction, then, of a cross-in-square plan with small outer chapels flanking the prothesis and diaconicon; access to the eastern roof chapels could have been along exterior wooden galleries.

Megaw's report was supplemented with a contribution by Mango and Hawkins which discusses the sculpture of both the north and south church and defines with greater accuracy our historical evidence about the founders of both churches. Other discussions of the sculpture have also appeared, Grabar dealing with the tenth century material, Wessel and Belting with the Palaeologan material.

Bibliography

Van Millingen, *Byzantine Churches*, pp. 122–37.

Ebersolt and Thiers, *Les églises*, pp. 211–13.

N. Brunov, "Ein Denkmal der Hofbaukunst von Konstantinopel," *Belvedere* 51–52 (1926), 217–36.

N. Brunov, "L'église à croix inscrite a cinq nefs dans l'architecture byzantine," *EO* 26 (1927), 257–86.

A.H.S. Megaw, "Notes on Recent Work of the Byzantine Institute in Istanbul," *DOP* 17 (1963), 333–35.

A. Grabar, *Sculptures byzantines de Constantinople* (Paris, 1963), pp. 100–122.

T. Macridy, "The Monastery of Lips and the Burials of the Palaeologi," *DOP* 18 (1964), 253–78.

A.H.S. Megaw, "The Original Form of the Theotokos Church of Constantine Lips," *DOP* 18 (1964), 279–98.

C. Mango and E.J.W. Hawkins, "Additional Notes on the Monastery of Lips," *DOP* 18 (1964), 299–315.

K. Wessel, "Byzantinische Plastik der palaiologischen Periode," *Byzantion* 36 (1966), 217–59.

Janin, *La géographie*, pp. 307–10, 417–18.

H. Belting, "Zur Skulptur aus der zeit um 1300 in Konstantinopel," *Münchener Jahrbuch der Bildenden Kunst* 23 (1972), 3, 63–100.

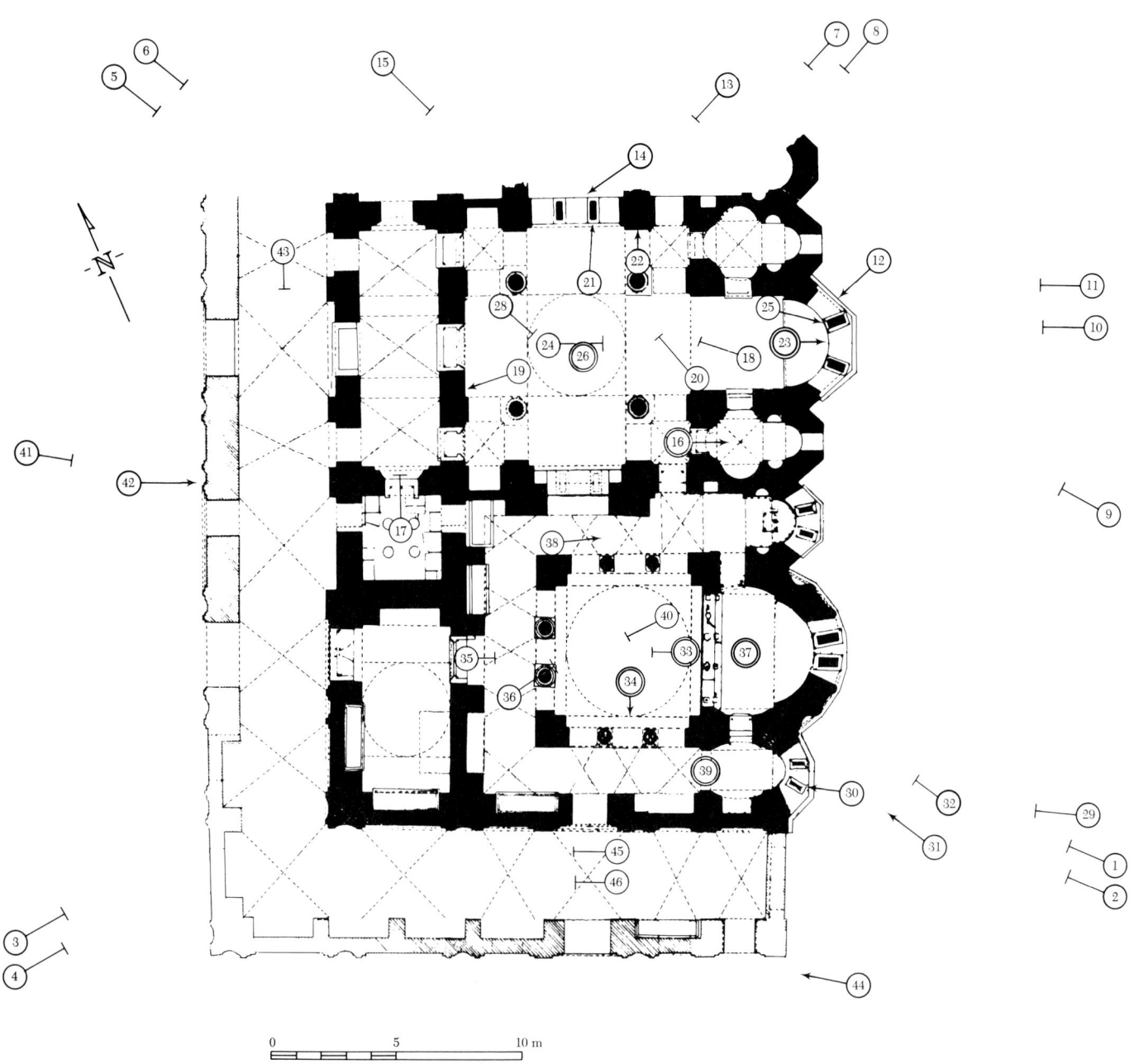

324 Theotokos tou Libos

35-1

35-2

35-1 General view from the southeast in 1955. Photo Hamann-MacLean, Bildarchiv Foto Marburg, 229142

35-2 General view from the southeast in its present state. M8107

35-3

35-4

35-5

35-3 General view from the southwest, c. 1925. A.K. Porter Collection, 1205, the Fogg Art Museum, Harvard University
35-4 General view from the southwest, in its present state. M15438
35-5 General view from above, from the northwest, in 1956. Photo Dumbarton Oaks Field Committee, H 56–68
35-6 General view from above, from the northwest, in its present state. M17333
35-7 General view from the northeast, c. 1925. A.K. Porter Collection, 1247, the Fogg Art Museum, Harvard University
35-8 General view from the northeast, in its present state. M20347

35-6

35-7

35-8

35-9

35-10

35-11

35-12

35-9   The north church from the southeast. M17268
35-10 The north church: the east end in its present state. M8111
35-11 The north church: the east end in 1955. Photo Hamann-MacLean, Bildarchiv Foto Marburg, 229143
35-12 The north church: detail of the inscription on the central apse. M8153

35-13 The north church: the north flank from the northeast. M20371

35-14

35-15

35-16

35-17

35-14 The north church: window capitals in the north wall. M20434
35-15 The north church: the north flank from the northwest. M20401
35-16 The north church: the southeast roof chapel during the restoration in 1959. Photo Dumbarton Oaks Field Committee, H 59.463
35-17 The north church: the inner narthex from the south. M8163

35-18

35-19

35-18 The north church: general interior view from the east. M8177
35-19 The north church: detail of the lower cornice on the west wall. M8242

35-20

35-21

35-22

35-20 The north church: the north wall from the sanctuary. M8206

35-21 The north church: detail of a window mullion in the north wall. Photo Dumbarton Oaks Field Committee, H 64-9

35-22 The north church: the east pier capital (reused) in the north wall. M8230

Theotokos tou Libos   333

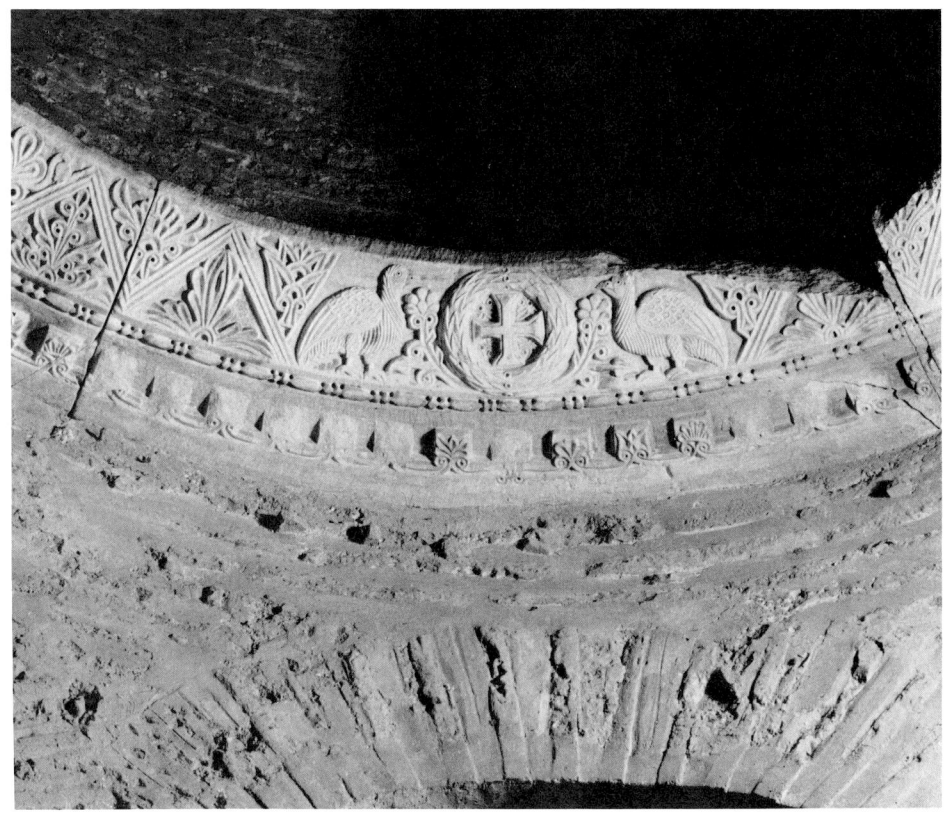

35-23

35-24

35-25

334 Theotokos tou Libos

35-26

35-27

35-23 The north church: detail of the cornice in the sanctuary. Photo Dumbarton Oaks Field Committee, H 62.313
35-24 The north church: view toward the sanctuary. M8165
35-25 The north church: the base of the north mullion in the sanctuary window. M8218
35-26 The north church: the pendentives and the cupola (Turkish above the cornice) with the east below. M8222
35-27 The north church: a fragment of the cornice of the dome. Photo Dumbarton Oaks Field Committee, H 62.10
35-28 The north church: the south wall. M8169

35-28

Theotokos tou Libos 335

35-29

35-30

35-31

35-29 The south church: view from above from the southeast. M17262
35-30 The south church: the south window mullion in the apse of the diaconicon. M20524
35-31 The south church: the main apse and diaconicon in 1955, before restoration. Photo Hamann-MacLean, Bildarchiv Foto Marburg, LA 1315145

35-32 The south church: the main apse and diaconicon in its present state. M8105

35-33

35-33 The south church: the upper parts of the church, from the east, in 1956 before restoration. Photo Dumbarton Oaks Field Committee, H 56.100
35-34 The south church: detail of the cornice of the cupola over the south arch. Photo Dumbarton Oaks Field Committee, H 62.88
35-35 The south church: view toward the sanctuary. M8258
35-36 The south church: the north wall with a view into the north ambulatory. M8260

35-34

35-35

35-36

Theotokos tou Libos 339

35-37

35-37 The south church: the vaulting in the sanctuary. M8274
35-38 The south church: the north ambulatory and the prothesis chapel. M8266
35-39 The south church: the vaulting in the diaconicon. M9813
35-40 The south church: view toward the western ambulatory and narthex. M8278

35-38

35-39

35-40

35-41

35-41 The outer narthex: west façade. M9608
35-42 The outer narthex: masonry detail of the west façade, showing the fourth niche from the north. M9733
35-43 The outer narthex: interior view from the north. M8159

35-42

35-43

35-44

35-44 The outer south aisle from the southeast. M9535
35-45 The outer south aisle, interior view from the east showing the original vaulting in c. 1940. Photo Eski Eserleri Koruma Encümeni, 3638, Istanbul Archaeological Museum
35-46 The outer south aisle, interior view from the east in its present state. M8214

344   Theotokos tou Libos

35-45

35-46

36

Theotokos hē Pammakaristos (The Mother-of-God the All-Blessed), and Christos ho Logos (Christ the Word). Fethiye Camii.

On its conversion to a mosque in 1586 the main church of the Pammakaristos was severely modified. The triple arcades which originally separated the square nave from the ambulatories on three sides were removed and broad pointed arches were substituted; the three apses were destroyed and in their place a domed square room was set obliquely against the eastern end of the building; fenestration was revised and the walls and piers were hewn back or remade to provide the maximum openness of space in the building. The end result leaves the original design difficult to recognize or appreciate. The parekklesion to the south, on the other hand, especially since its cleaning and restoration by the Byzantine Institute of the United States and by Dumbarton Oaks, is one of Constantinople's most impressive monuments, notwithstanding its small scale. Jewel-like in its colorful surface patterns and careful workmanship, it is the finest example of Palaeologan architecture in the capital. The plan is the classic cross-in-square, but it is developed here with new steeper proportions, raising the level of the cross element a story above the vaulting of the sanctuary. Only fragments of the polychrome revetment remain, but many of the mosaics, works of outstanding quality, are still intact.

The bibliography on the Pammakaristos is not very satisfactory. Underwood and Megaw prepared preliminary articles describing the process of cleaning the parekklesion and its mosaics, but as a whole the mosaics are still unreported and unknown. On the complicated issues of the building phase of the main church, two studies were published almost simultaneously, one by Hallensleben and the other by Mango and Hawkins, with somewhat different conclusions.

Although the continued Christian use of the church as the seat of the Patriarch from 1455 to 1586 has given us an especially rich documentation on the history of the church—material first published by Siderides—the original foundation of the main church is still unknown. It is true that the gap has narrowed considerably since Van Millingen and Ebersolt proposed the eighth and the thirteenth century, respectively. The archaeology of Mango, Hawkins, and Hallensleben leaves no doubt that the building is Comnenian, with typical recessed brickwork in both the cistern underneath and the church proper. But it is difficult to narrow the span further. Hallensleben assigned the main church to the mid-eleventh century on the basis of its dedicatory inscription; but Mango and Hawkins point out that the "John Comnenus" named in the inscription could be any of several different historical figures. Instead, they propose that the niches which articulate the exterior wall of the narthex point to a late twelfth century date. There is also disagreement on the date of the addition of the outer north aisle. Mango and Hawkins assign it to the same period as the outer narthex and outer south aisle; but prerestoration photographs seem to bear out Hallensleben's belief that it was earlier.

We are much better informed about the date and circumstances of the erection of the parekklesion, which was dedicated by Martha Glabas to her late husband Michael shortly after 1310. The poet Philes was asked to compose the inscription addressed to Christ the Word that ran both inside and outside the building. Apparently the main church was also refurbished at this time, for the fragments of its templon seem to belong to the early fourteenth century; the fragments were discussed by Mango and Hawkins and again by Belting.

Bibliography

A. Siderides, "Peri tēs en Kōnstantinoupolei monēs tēs Pammakaristou," *Hellēnikos philologikos syllogos* suppl. to vol. 20-22 (1892), 19-32; 29 (1907), 265-73.

Van Millingen, *Byzantine Churches*, pp. 138-63.

Ebersolt and Thiers, *Les églises*, pp. 225-47.

P.A. Underwood, "Notes on the Work of the Byzantine Institute in Istanbul," *DOP* 9-10 (1956), 298-99; 14 (1960), 215-19.

A. Megaw, "Notes on Recent Work of the Byzantine Institute," *DOP* 17 (1963), 367-71.

C. Mango and E. Hawkins, "Report on Field Work in Istanbul and Cyprus, 1962-63," *DOP* 18 (1964), 319-33.

H. Hallensleben, "Untersuchungen zur Baugeschichte der ebemaligen Pammakaristos-kirche, der heutigen Fethiye Camii, in Istanbul," *IM* 13-14 (1963-64), 128-93.

Janin, *La géographie*, pp. 208-13.

P. Schreiner, "Eine unbekannte Beschreibung der Pammakaristos-kirche (Fethiye Camii) und weitere Texte zur Topographie Konstantinopels," *DOP* 25 (1971), 217-48.

H. Belting, "Zur Skulptur aus der zeit um 1300 in Konstantinopel," *Münchener Jahrbuch der Bildenden Kunst* 23 (1972), 3, 63-100.

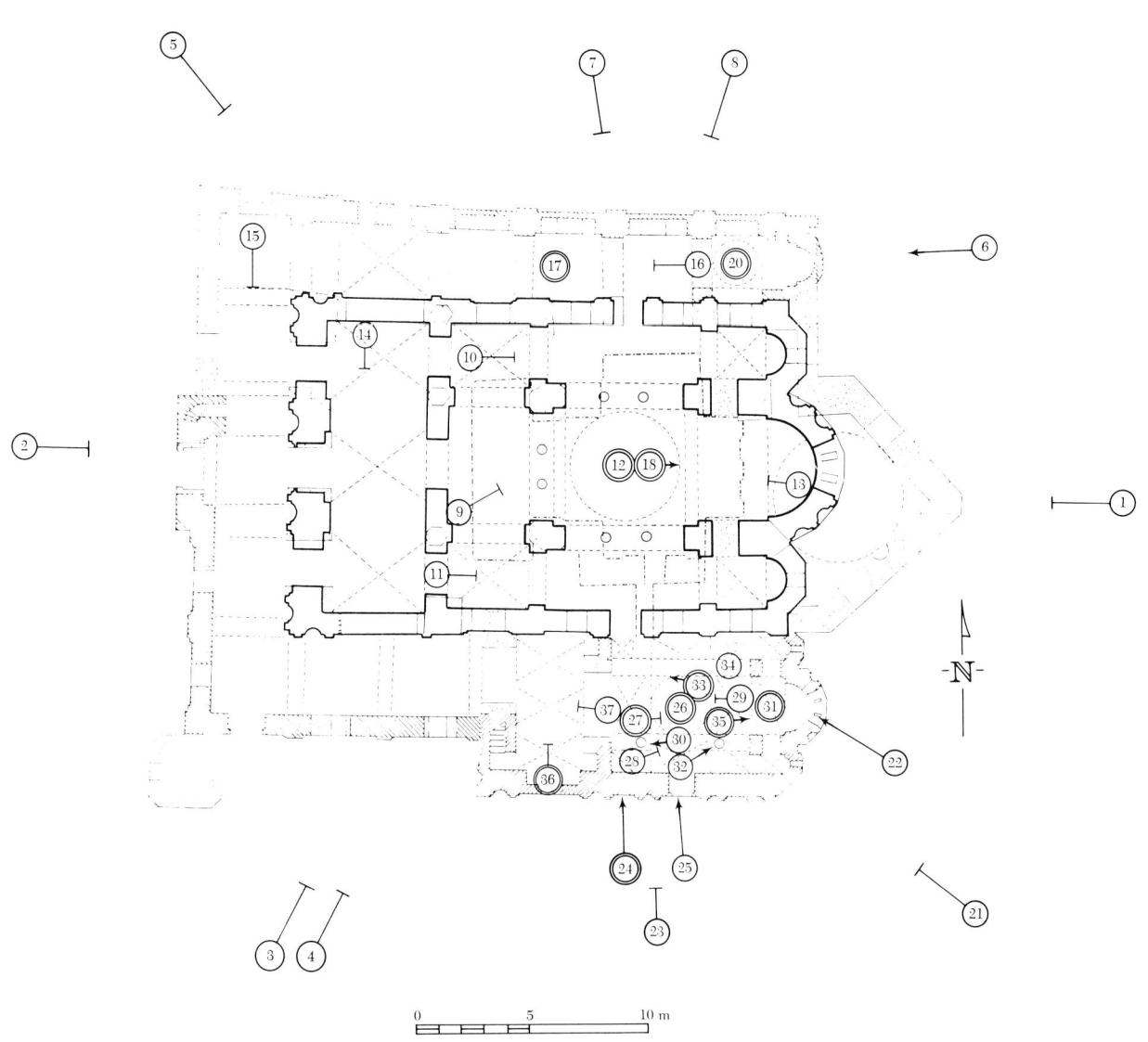

from Mango

348 Theotokos hē Pammakaristos

36-1

36-2

36-1   General view from the east. M13946
36-2   General view from the west. M17605

Theotokos hē Pammakaristos

36-3

350 Theotokos hē Pammakaristos

36-4

36-3 General view from the southwest at present. M2613
36-4 General view from the southwest, c. 1938. Photo Eski Eserleri Koruma Encümeni, 2241, Istanbul Archaeological Museum

36-5

36-6

36-7

36-5 General view from the northwest. M17004
36-6 The main church: the outer north chapel from the east. M15528
36-7 The main church from the north, c. 1938. Photo Eski Eserleri Koruma Encümeni, 2242, Istanbul Archaeological Museum
36-8 The main church from the north. M15420

36-8

Theotokos hē Pammakaristos

36-9

36-10

36-11

36-9   The main church: a view into the nave from the west ambulatory. M16835
36-10   The main church: the north ambulatory from the west. M16832
36-11   The main church: the south ambulatory from the west. M16842
36-12   The main church: the cupola and adjacent vaulting, with the east below. M16729
36-13   The main church: a view into the nave from the sanctuary, in 1957. Photo Dumbarton Oaks Field Committee, H.57.904
36-14   The main church: the inner narthex from the north. M16850

36-12

36-13

36-14

36-15

36-16

36-17

36-20

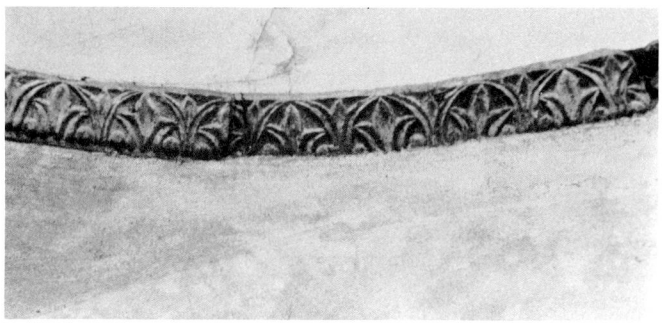

36-18

36-19

36-15 The main church: the outer narthex from the north, in 1957. Photo Dumbarton Oaks Field Committee, H.57.836

36-16 The main church: the outer north aisle from the east, in 1957. Photo Dumbarton Oaks Field Committee, H.57.807

36-17 The main church: domical vaulting in the fourth bay from the east, of the outer north aisle, with the south below. H.57.822

36-18 The main church: a detail of the cornice under the drum of the main dome, section over the eastern arch. M16870

36-19 The main church: relief of an Apostle, probably from the templon, now in the museum of Hagia Sophia. M10903

36-20 The main church: cupola over the easternmost bay of the outer north aisle, with the east below. M16760

36-21

Theotokos hē Pammakaristos

36-22

36-23

36-24

36-25

36-21 The parekklesion from the southeast. M2536A
36-22 The parekklesion: mullion and capital in the apse window. M2605
36-23 The parekklesion: the south flank from the south. M2534
36-24 The parekklesion: detail of decorative brickwork in the south flank. M20968
36-25 The parekklesion: the lower window in the south crossarm. M7611

36-26 The parekklesion: the vaulting of the cupola and crossarms, with the east below. M27528

36-27 The parekklesion: the vaulting of the cupola, crossarms, and apse. M27536

36-28

36-29

36-30

36-31

36-28 The parekklesion: the sanctuary and the diaconicon from the west. M3805
36-29 The parekklesion: general view from the east. M3826
36-30 The parekklesion: the southwest capital and the vaulting in the southwest corner bay. M7615
36-31 The parekklesion: the vaulting of the apse. M3819

36-32

36-33

36-34

36-35

364 Theotokos hē Pammakaristos

36-36

36-37

36-32 The parekklesion: the southeast capital. M27630
36-33 The parekklesion: detail of the cornice under the drum, over the northwest pendentive. M27607
36-34 The parekklesion: fragment of pavement in the northeast corner. M7635
36-35 The parekklesion: detail of the marble revetment over the eastern arch. M27624
36-36 The parekklesion: the vaulting of the narthex from the south. M7643
36-37 The parekklesion: the narthex and outer south aisle from the east. M7627

37

Theotokos hē Panagiotissa (The Mother-of-God the All-Holy). Theotokos Panagia Mougliotissa (The All-Holy Mother-of-God of the Mongols). Kanlī Kilise.

The fact that the Panagiotissa has remained in use as an Orthodox church down to the present—unique among the Byzantine churches of the city—has been a mixed blessing to historical research on the monument. For although it assures us of the correct historical identification of the monument, it has until now prevented any serious study of the architecture. Thoroughly covered with plaster, critical evidence of the masonry types, or the joints and phases of construction, remains beyond our inspection. In addition, it is to its Metabyzantine use as a church that one must attribute the most serious mutilation of the structure, the destruction of the south apse and the addition of an incongruous double-naved hall on this side of the church.

The shape of the original design, however, can be easily distinguished from the later additions, and this was the contribution of the earliest studies of the building, those of Gurlitt, Van Millingen, and Brunov. The church was first erected as a simple quatrefoil with neither pastophoria nor narthex. Bettini's suggestion that the narthex, whose northern and central bays still stand, was part of the original plan does not agree with the evident mutilations of the quatrefoil in accommodating the construction of the narthex. The interior of the original quatrefoil core was enlivened with three long, steep niches in each apse and columns at the corners between the apses (only two of the latter remain and they are hidden by the iconostasis). The three-bay narthex was then added later, possibly in Palaeologan times when many of the city's churches received new nartheces. The hall to the south of the church, a belfry and porch in front of the narthex, and a high wall enclosing the whole precinct to the front and south of the church are all modern additions. A sculptured relief of Christ Emmanuel, of Palaeologan workmanship, has been mounted in the precinct wall facing the entrance to the church.

The date of the church is still a problem. The name Mougliotissa, or "Mongolian," was attached to the monastery in honor of its thirteenth-century benefactress Maria Palaeologina, daughter of Michael VIII and wife of a Mongolian prince, and this has led historians traditionally to see the church as a thirteenth century building. But new evidence brought forward by Kougeas and Laurent indicates that the sanctuary and monastery of the Panagiotissa, or of tōn Panagiou, was already in existence in the eleventh and possibly even in the tenth century. Whether the present church dates from that early a period is a question that only archaeology can settle finally, but a comparison of the monument with the other two narthex-less quatrefoils in the immediate vicinity, the Panagia Kamariotissa on Heybeliada and the no longer extant Sinaitikon in Edirne, would favor the earlier date.

Bibliography

C. Gurlitt, *Die Baukunst Konstantinopels* (Berlin, 1912), pp. 36–37.

Van Millingen, *Byzantine Churches,* pp. 272–79.

N. Brunov, "Die Panagia-Kirche auf der Insel Chalki in der Umgebung von Konstantinopel," *Byz-Neugriechische Jarbücher* 6 (1927–28), 509–20.

S. Bettini, "Un inedito mosaico del periodo paleologo a Constantinopoli," *Atti del V Congresso di studi bizantini* 2. *Studi bizantini e neoellenici,* 6 (Rome, 1940), 31–36.

S. Kougeas, "Ho Geōrgios Akropolitēs ktētōr tou Parisinou kōdikos tou Souïda," *Byzantina Metabyzantina,* 1949, 61–74.

V. Laurent, *Le corpus des sceaux de l'empire byzantin,* V, 2: *L'église* (Paris, 1965), pp. 94–96.

Janin, *La géographie,* pp. 213–14.

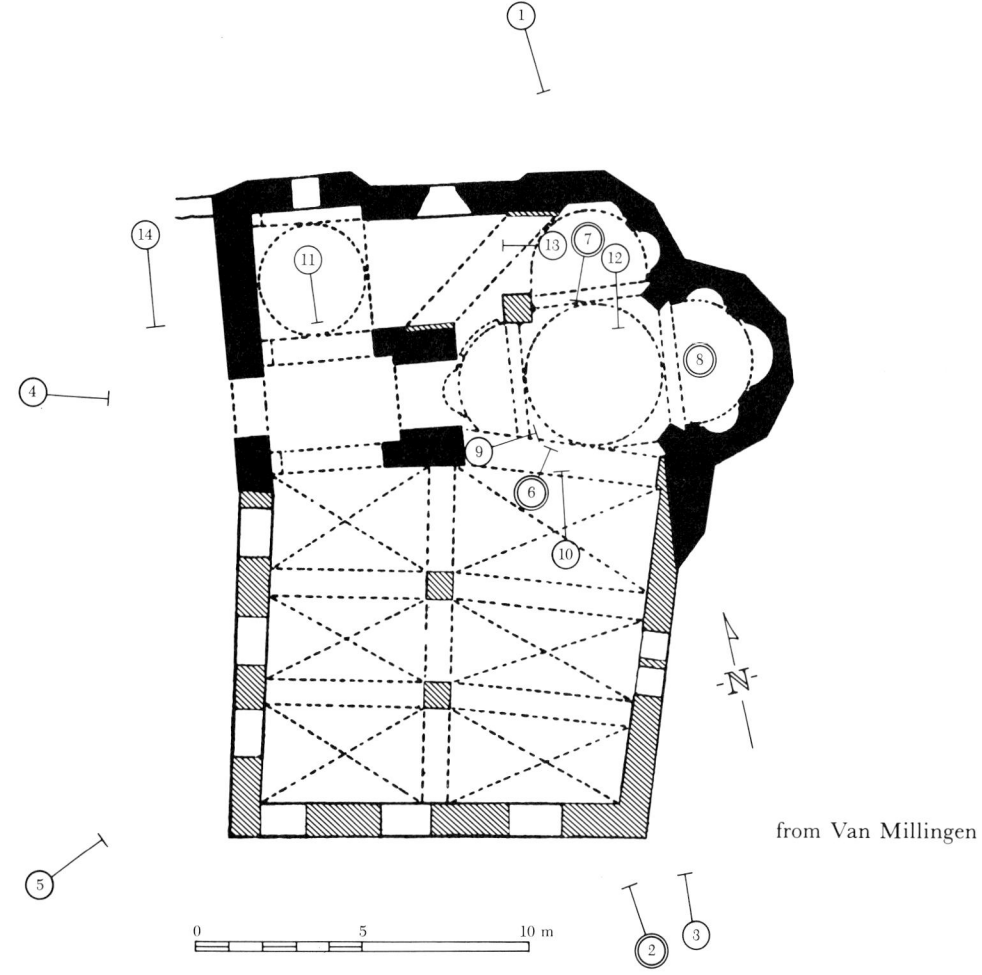

from Van Millingen

37 1

37-1 General view from the north. M13636
37-2 General view from above, from the south. M13968
37-3 View from the south. M2521

Theotokos hē Panagiotissa

37-2

37-3

Theotokos hē Panagiotissa

37-4

37-5

37-4 General view of the church and its precinct area from the west, from Paspates' lithograph, 1877
37-5 The west façade from the southwest, with the outer narthex and belfry. M13504
37-6 View of the vaulting from the southwest. M13602

370   Theotokos hē Panagiotissa

37-6

37-7

372 Theotokos hē Panagiotissa

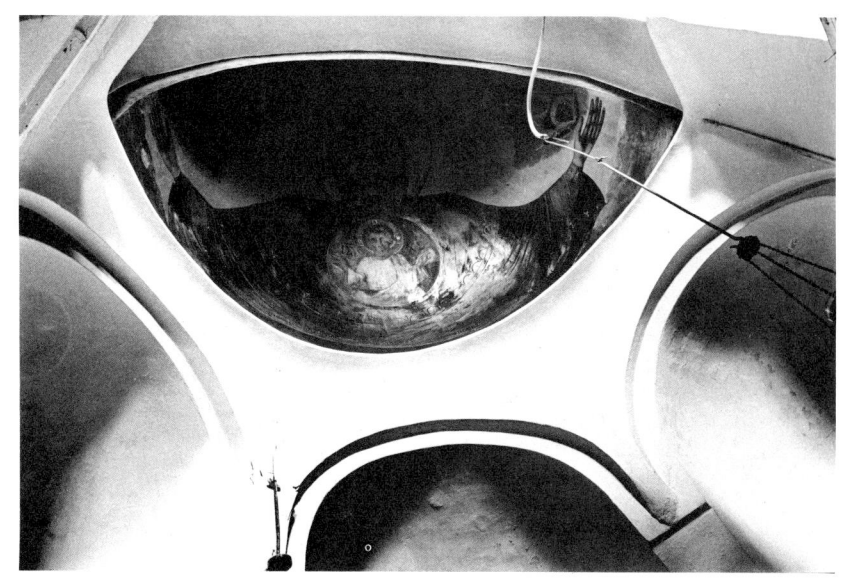

37-8

37-7 View of the vaulting from the north apse. M13526
37-8 Vaulting in the east apse. M13529
37-9 The east apse and the iconostasis from the southwest. M13821

37-9

37-10

37-11

37-12

37-13

374   Theotokos hē Panagiotissa

37-14

37-15

37-10 The north apse and part of the west apse from the south. M13606
37-11 The narthex from the north. M13621
37-12 The south hall from the north. M13533
37-13 The north aisle from the east. M13617
37-14 The outer narthex from the north. M13629
37-15 Relief of Christ Emmanuel in the atrium wall. M13815

38

Toklu Dede Mescidi

Apart from the replacement of the vaulting of nave and narthex with low-pitched timber roofs, this little church remained practically intact until 1929 when it was sold for demolition as a source of building materials. By the time museum authorities intervened to save it nothing remained but the south wall and half of the apse. It was at this stage that Janin observed the monument, and that Schneider studied and recorded the remains of the frescoes—a fourteenth century cycle including a series of individual saints with a Nativity in the sanctuary. Since that time, the apse and the frescoes and the upper half of the south wall have also disappeared, though enough still remained in 1954 to permit Pasadaios to make some fresh observations and to reconstruct the elevation. Pasadaios's plan represents a considerable gain in accuracy over Van Millingen's, but at the same time it contains a number of errors of detail. The most accurate measurements of the building are found in the unpublished plan of the Eski Eserleri Koruma Encümeni prepared in 1923; that plan served as basis for the one included here.

The church was unusually simple in design. It consisted only of a domed nave approximately 5 meters square, preceded by a narthex on the west and opening eastward into a barrel-vaulted sanctuary. The sanctuary had the traditional prothesis and diaconicon, but reduced in size to mere shallow, decorative niches flanking the apse.

The exterior articulation of the apse of the Toklu Dede dates the building securely in the eleventh or early twelfth century. The squat niches over the windows are akin to those of several other churches known to be eleventh century foundations, including the Pantepoptēs and the Vefa Kilise Camii; and the brick corbel frieze finds its parallel at the Gül Camii. This date would be consistent with Van Millingen's identification of the church as Hag. Thekla, which was part of the Blachernēs Palace, built by Isaac and John II Comnenus; but Van Millingen's hypothesis is open to doubt on other scores. In the first place his derivation of "Toklu" from "Thekla" is unfounded; moreover, we have no evidence that the Blachernēs Palace extended this far down the Golden Horn. Eyice's suggested identification as Hag. Priskos kai Nikolaos is untenable, since it presumes a sixth century date for the church.

Bibliography

Van Millingen, *Byzantine Churches,* pp. 207–11.

A.M. Schneider, "Die byzantinischen Fresken der Toklu Dede Mescidi," *AA* (1930), 443–44; reprinted in *Byzanz,* pp. 15–16.

R. Janin, "La topographie de Constantinople byzantine: études et découvertes, 1918–38," *EO* 38 (1939), 143–44; *La géographie,* p. 141.

S. Eyice, *Istanbul, Petit guide,* pp. 66–67.

A. Pasadaios, "To pheron epōnymian Toklou Ibrahēm Dede Mescidi byzantinon ktērion," *Archēologikē Ephēmeris* (1969), 80–124.

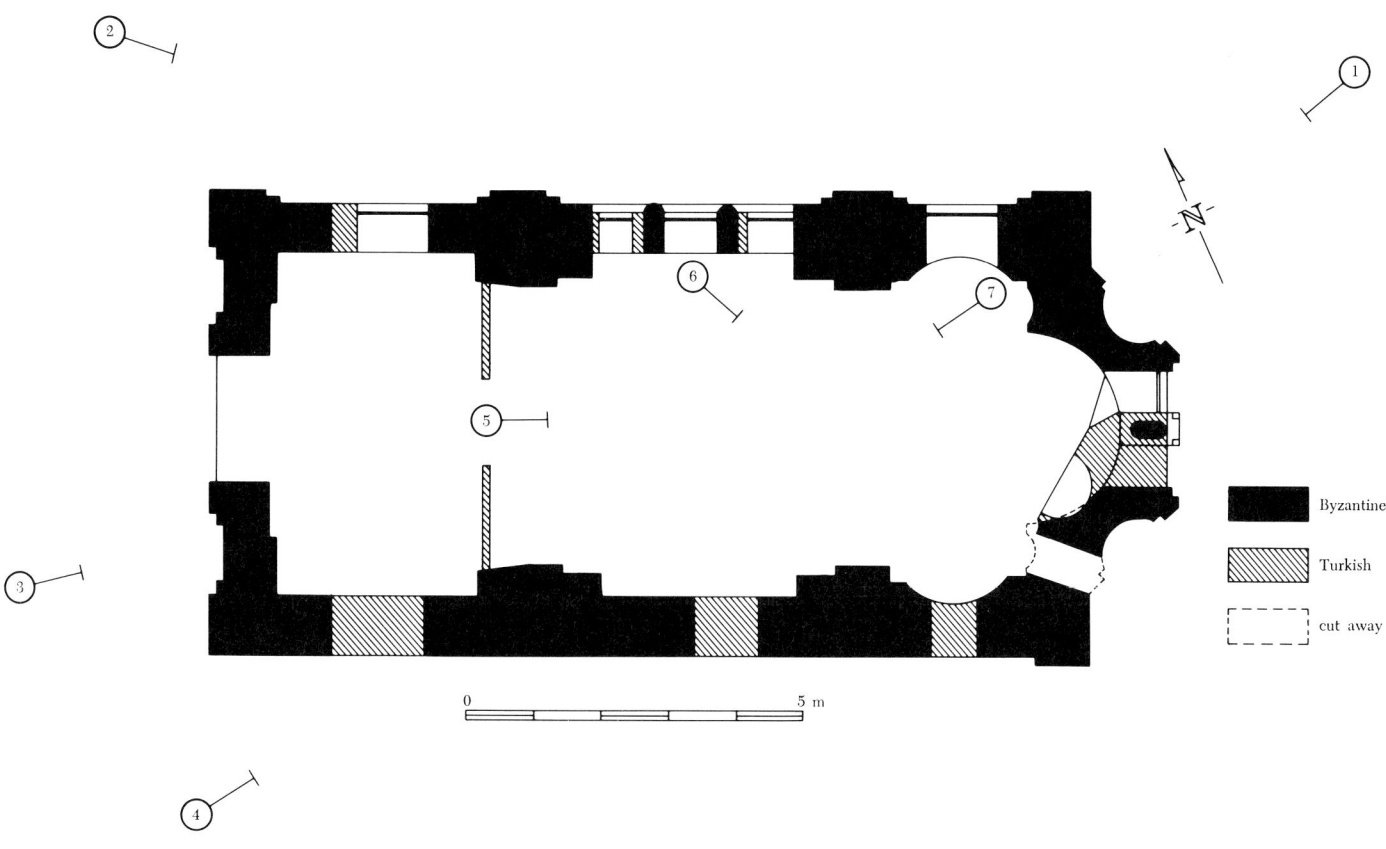

Mathews

38-1

38-2

38-1 The apse from the east, c. 1923. Eski Eserleri Koruma Encümeni, 109, Istanbul Archaeological Museum

38-2 The north flank of the church from the northwest, c. 1923. Eski Eserleri Koruma Encümeni, 108, Istanbul Archaeological Museum

38-3

38-4

38-5

38-3 The west façade, before 1929. Photo Sender, rephotographed. M22417
38-4 The south flank of the church from the southwest, in 1949. Dumbarton Oaks Field Committee, L49.183
38-5 Sanctuary interior, c. 1923. Eski Eserleri Koruma Encümeni, 110, Istanbul Archaeological Museum

38-6

38-7

38-6 Sanctuary with fresco remains, c. 1936. Photo Artamonoff, Dumbarton Oaks Field Committee, RA 360

38-7 Remains of the south wall in its present state, from the northeast. M21626

39

Topkapı Sarayı Basilica

The smallest of the early basilicas of Constantinople, the Topkapı Sarayı church, which was found beneath the second courtyard of the sultan's palace, is also the least well known of the group. The remains of the monument were uncovered in 1937 by Ogan, then director of the Archeological Museum, with the collaboration of Bossert; but the site was subsequently covered over again, leaving the sketchy reports of the archaeologists as our only first-hand evidence. The main features, however, are well established and these differ from the plans of the other basilicas in some important respects.

Like the Chalkoprateia and the Stoudios basilicas, the Topkapı church consisted of a nave flanked by aisles making an interior of almost square proportions. The forecourt that preceded the building, however, lay off axis, partly west and partly north of the church, and the main entrance was through the north door of the narthex. The disposition of the east end of the church was also somewhat unusual. The sanctuary, instead of occupying the easternmost part of the nave, was added on east of the nave in a short rectangular bay, terminating in an apse. Schneider's attempt to read this feature as a transept is not convincing. In front of the sanctuary were found indications of an ambo and a solea, the earliest archaeological evidence of these furnishings in Constantinople.

The dedication of the Topkapı Sarayı basilica remains unknown, and the dating cannot be fixed with any greater precision than the mid-fifth century. The architectural sculpture, the *opus sectile* pavement, and the coin finds all point in this direction, but unfortunately they were not reported on carefully enough to yield more information. A find of tenth and eleventh century tiles, reported on by Ettinghausen, indicates that the church was redecorated in Middle Byzantine times. A small apsed chapel was found 50 meters south of the church and other Christian remains in the vicinity have been noticed.

Bibliography

A.M. Schneider, "Grabung im Hof des Top Kapi sarayi," *Jahrbuch des deutschen archäologischen Instituts* 54 (1939), 179–82.

H.T. Bossert, "Istanbul Akropolunde Üniversite Hafriyatı," *Üniversite Konferansları* 125 (1939–40), 206–31.

A. Ogan, "Les fouilles de Topkapu Saray enterprises en 1937 par la Societé d'histoire Turque," *Belleten* 4 (1940), 318–35.

E. Mamboury, "Les fouilles byzantines à Istanbul et ses environs," *Byzantion* 21 (1951), 426–27.

E. Ettinghausen, "Byzantine Tiles from the Basilica in the Topkapu Sarayi and Saint John of Stoudios," *CA* 7 (1954), 79–88.

Mathews, *The Early Churches of Constantinople,* pp. 33–38.

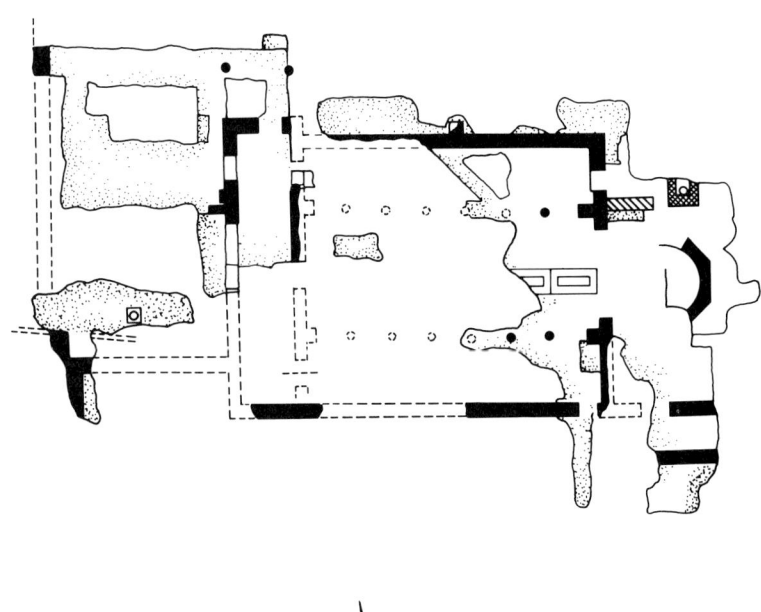

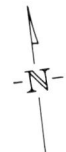

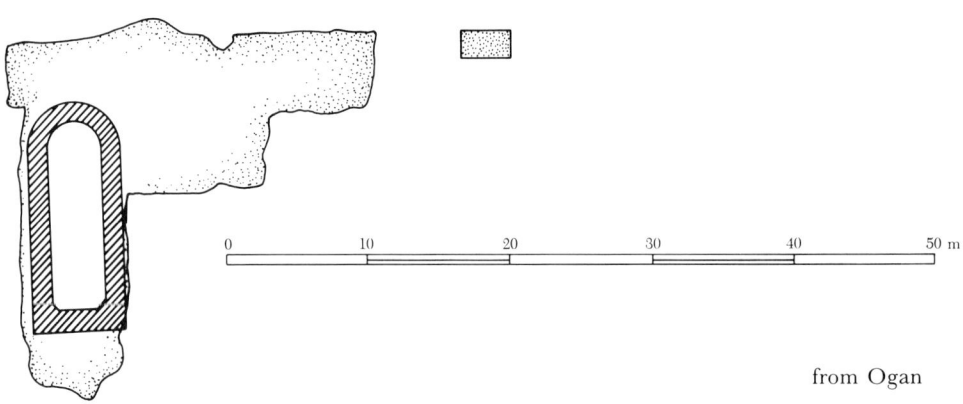

from Ogan

39-1

39-2

39-3

39-1 Opus sectile pavement. Photo A. Ogan
39-2 Pilaster capital from church. Photo A. Ogan
39-3 Fragments of a screen from the church. Photo A. Ogan

40

Vefa Kilise Camii

The Vefa Kilise Camii has never been subjected to any systematic overall study and the building presents many unresolved problems. In the first place the original identity of the monument is unknown. Despite the efforts of earlier Byzantinists to assign a Christian name, Hag. Theodoros, the topographical data in the sources are quite inconclusive, as Janin indicated. In the second place, the date of the monument is known only in general terms and scholarship has not advanced much beyond the observations of Ebersolt and Van Millingen in this respect. The design of the east end of the church proper places the core on the building in the eleventh or early twelfth century, while the banded brickwork and stonework of the outer narthex and its complex arcaded façade belong sometime in the Palaeologan period. Later than the outer narthex, but also otherwise undated, is the two-story annex which was added on the north flank of the church, like the annex at the Chōra church.

Even the plan of the Vefa Kilise Camii presents a problem. Texier and other nineteenth century archaeologists have left us drawings showing that the south arm of the quincunx plan used to open through a triple arcade into an outer chapel that lay along the south flank of the church. On this basis Brunov proposed that the church was originally built on a "five-aisled" plan—that is, it had outer aisles on both north and south, giving the church a five-apsed east end. On the north side, however, photographs taken before this part of the church was restored show that the present northeast corner is the original exterior corner of the building, and therefore if an outer north aisle existed it could have been only as an addition to the original plan. Hallensleben has recently proposed that the outer south aisle was, in fact, an addition, a porch of Palaeologan date terminating in a little parekklesion at the east. Unfortunately all evidence for the outer south aisle was obliterated in modern restoration and the question cannot be solved without excavating the site. Hallensleben's other suggestion, that the square chamber southeast of the minaret is the first story of a belfry belonging to the same building phase as the outer narthex, is quite reasonable in view of the massive walls of this chamber.

Elements of the church's decoration can still be seen in the outer narthex. The architectural sculpture of columns, capitals, and closure slabs was all reused material of Early Byzantine origin. The three domes were covered with mosaics, and those of the south dome have survived in a reasonably complete state and were cleaned in 1937 under the direction of the Ministry of Mosques. The interior of the church proper, however, has never been stripped of its plaster.

Bibliography

Van Millingen, *Byzantine Churches*, pp. 243–52.

Ebersolt and Thiers, *Les églises*, pp. 149–56.

N. Brunov, "Über zwei byzantinische Baudenkmäler von Konstantinopel aus dem XI. Jahrhundert," *Byzantinisch-Neugriechische Jahrbücher* 9 (1931–32), 139–44.

R. Janin, "La topographie de Constantinople byzantine: études et découvertes, 1918–38," *EO* 38 (1939), 138–39.

Eyice, *Son devir Bizans Mimarisi*, pp. 47–50.

H. Hallensleben, "Zu Annexbauten der Kilise camii in Istanbul," *IM* 15 (1965), 208–17.

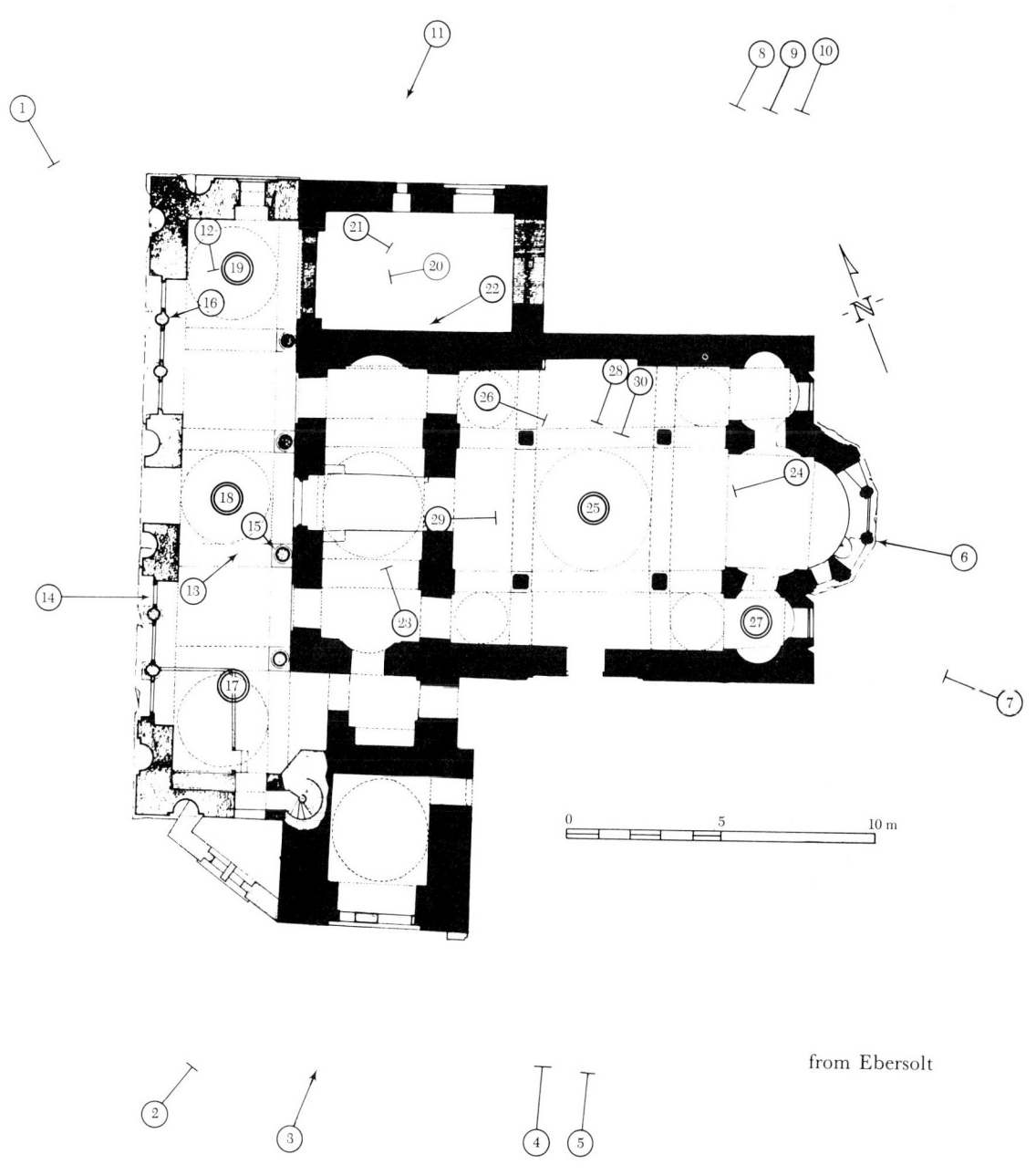

from Ebersolt

40-1

40-2

40-3

40-1 The west façade from the northwest. M12906A
40-2 General view from the southwest. M10211
40-3 Detail of the south flank showing the remaining first story of the tower, in 1950. Photo Josephine Powell, T 10–2

40-4

40-5

40-6

390　Vefa Kilise Camii

40-7

40-4 The south flank of the church as drawn by Texier, c. 1835. Photo Royal Institute of British Architects
40-5 The south flank of the church. M21314
40-6 Colonette and capital in the apse. M8055
40-7 View from the southeast. Photo Schiele, German Archaeological Institute, Istanbul, R3294

40-8

40-9

40-10

40-8 Detail of the north flank of the church from the northeast, c. 1920. Photo A.K. Porter Collection, 5377, the Fogg Art Museum, Harvard
40-9 The north flank of the church from the northeast, 1950. Photo Josephine Powell T 10-1
40-10 The north flank of the church from the northeast in its present state. M25807
40-11 Detail of the north flank, showing the north annex and the outer narthex. M6002

40-11

40-12

394 Vefa Kilise Camii

40-13

40-14

40-15

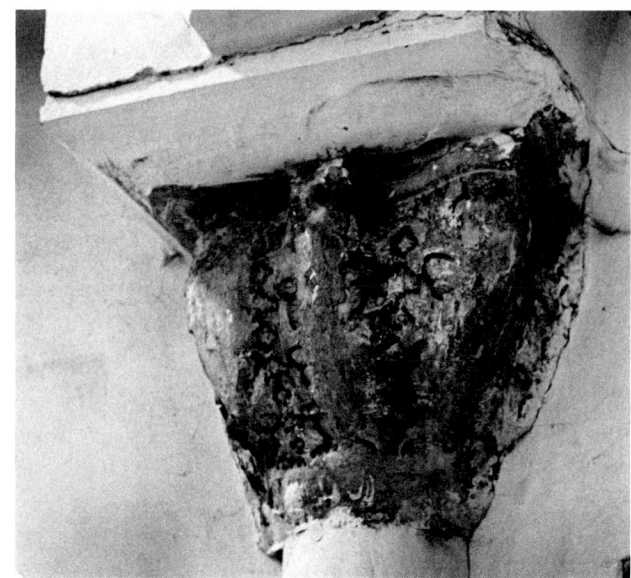

40-16

40-12 The outer narthex from the north. M27221
40-13 The door leading from the outer to the inner narthex. M7949
40-14 A relief slab (the third from the south) in the arcade of the façade. M8067
40-15 Capital to the right of the door in 40-13. M7969
40-16 The northernmost capital, unfinished, in the west wall of the outer narthex. M8015

40-17

40-18

40-19

40-17 The south cupola of the outer narthex and the neighboring vault to the north. M27229
40-18 The central cupola of the outer narthex, with the east below. M27333
40-19 The north cupola of the outer narthex, with the east below. M27330

40-20

40-21

40-22

40-23

40-20 The north annex, ground floor, from the east. M7961
40-21 The north annex, ground floor, from the west. M7965
40-22 Capital, extreme right in 40-21. M8011
40-23 The inner narthex from the south. M5822
40-24 General view of the interior from the east. M27313

40-24

Vefa Kilise Camii

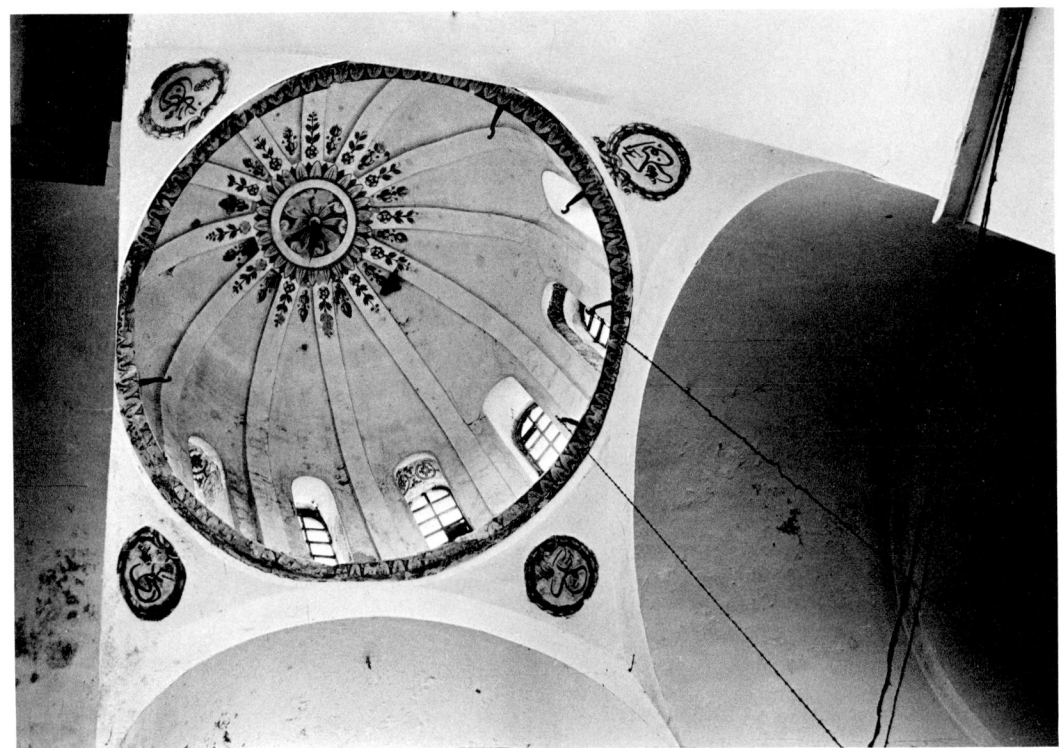

40-25

40-26

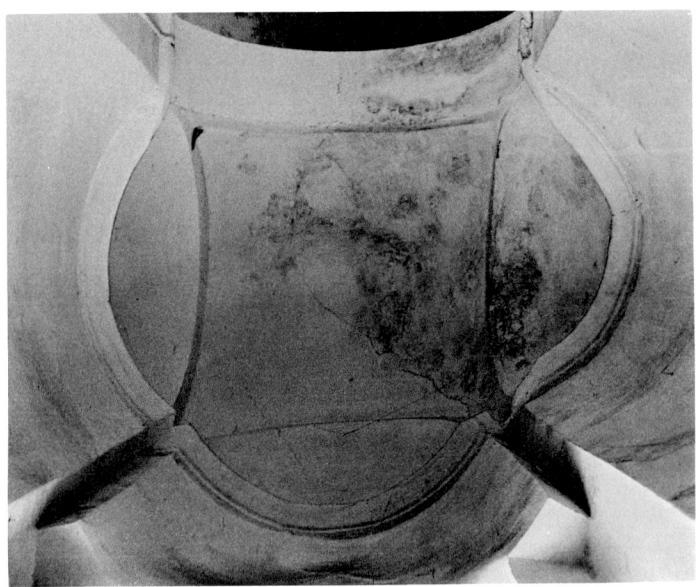

40-27

Vefa Kilise Camii

40-28

- *40-25* The dome and adjacent vaulting, with the sanctuary to the right. M6019
- *40-26* The sanctuary and prothesis chapel. M6017
- *40-27* Vaulting in the diaconicon. M6021
- *40-28* The arcade in the south wall opening into the parekklesion, as drawn by Texier, c. 1835. Photo Royal Institute of British Architects
- *40-29* View toward the sanctuary. M27235
- *40-30* The south wall in its present state. M27306

40-29

40-30

Index

Abdülmecit I, sultan, 263
Acem Ağa Mescidi, *see* Theotokos tōn Chalkoprateiōn
Ahmet Paşa Camii, *see* Iōannēs Prodromos en tō Troullō, Hag.
Alexius I Comnenus, emperor, 59, 200
Andreas en tē Krisei, Hag., 3-14, 15
Andrew, St., *see* Andreas en tē Krisei, Hag.
Andronicus II, Palaeologus, emperor, 200
Anicia Juliana, 225
Anna Dalassena, 59
Anthemius of Tralles, 263, 264
Antiochus, praepositus, 123
Apostles, Holy, xvi
Arsenal Churches, *see* Mangana Churches
Atatürk, president, 264
Athos, Panteleimon, 36
Atik Mustafa Paşa Camii, 15-22
Ayasofya Camii, *see* Sophia, Hagia
Ayasofya Müzesi, *see* Sophia, Hagia
Aykapı Church, 23-24

Balaban Ağa Mescidi, 25-27
Baptistery: Beyazit B, 28; Hagia Sophia, 262, 264; Şeyh Süleyman Mescidi, 315; Theotokos tōn Chalkoprateiōn, 319
Basil I, emperor, 128, 319
Beyazit II, sultan, 40, 209
Beyazit Church D, 28, 34-35
Beyazit Churches A, B, and C, xvii, 28-33
Bogdan Sarayı, xvii, 36-39
Budrum Camii, *see* Myrelaion

Chalcedon, xvi
Chalcedon, Hag. Euphēmia, 123
Chōra, *see* Christos tēs Chōras
Christ the All-Ruler, *see* Christos ho Pantokratōr
Christ the All-Seeing, *see* Christos ho Pantepoptēs
Christ of Chōra, *see* Christos tēs Chōras
Christ the Word, *see* Theotokos hē Pammakaristos
Christos ho Akataleptos, 172
Christos tēs Chōras, 40-58, 168, 191
Christos tēs Kyras Marthas, 237
Christos ho Logos, *see* Theotokos hē Pammakaristos

Christos ho Pantepoptēs, 59-70, 313, 376
Christos ho Pantokratōr, 71-101, 171, 225, 315
Christos ho Philanthrōpos, 200
Constantine Lips, 322
Constantine Monomachus, emperor, 200
Constantius II, emperor, 262

Edirne, Sinaitikon, 366
Eirēnē, Hag., 102-22
Eski Imaret Camii, *see* Christos ho Pantepoptēs
Euphēmia en tō Hippodromō, Hag., 123-27, 200
Euphēmia en tō Petriō, Hag., 128
Euphemia, St., *see* Euphēmia en tō Hippodromō

Fenarî Isa Camii, *see* Theotokos tou Libos
Fethiye Camii, *see* Theotokos hē Pammakaristos
Forum Tauri, 25, 28
Francis Assisi, St., 172

Gastria monastery, 231
Geōrgios tōn Mananōn, 200
Golden Gate, 143
Gül Camii, 23, 128-39, 260, 376

Hagiasma: Beyazit B, 28; Mangana, 200-201
Hazreti Cabir Camii, *see* Atik Mustafa Paşa Camii
Hebdomon, xvi, 140
Heybeliada, Panagia Kamariotissa, xvii, 366
Hippodrome, 123, 242
Hırami Ahmet Paşa Camii, *see* Iōannēs Prodromos en tō Troullō, Hag.
Hodēgētria icon, 71, 201
Holy Peace, *see* Eirēnē, Hag.
Holy Wisdom, *see* Sophia, Hagia
Hormisdas palace, 242

Iakōbos, Hag., *see* Theotokos tōn Chalkoprateiōn
Ibrahim Paşa Mescidi, *see* Isa Kapısı Mescidi

Ilyas Bey Mescidi, *see* Iōannēs Prodromos en tois Stoudiou, Hag.
Imrahor Mescidi, *see* Iōannēs Prodromos en tois Stoudiou, Hag.
Iōannēs Prodromos en tō Hebdomō, 140–42
Iōannēs Prodromos tou Libos, Hag., *see* Theotokos tou Libos
Iōannēs Prodromos en tois Stoudiou, Hag., 143–58, 319, 383
Iōannēs Prodromos en tō Troullō, Hag., 159–67, 231, 237
Irene Choumnos, 200
Irene Comnenus, 71
Isaac Comnenus, 41, 376
Isa Kapısı Mescidi, 168–70
Isidore of Miletus, 263, 264

James, St., *see* Theotokos tōn Chalkoprateiōn
Jerusalem, Holy Sepulchre, 25
John II Comnenus, emperor, 71, 376
John the Forerunner at the Dome, St., *see* Iōannēs Prodromos en tō Troullō, Hag.
John the Forerunner in Hebdomon, St., *see* Iōannēs Prodromos en tō Hebdomō, Hag.
John the Forerunner of Lips, St., *see* Theotokos tou Libos
John the Forerunner in the Stoudios Estates, St., *see* Iōannēs Prodromos en tois Stoudiou, Hag.
Justinian I, emperor, 102, 140, 242, 263, 264

Kalenderhane Camii, 28, 171–85
Kanlı Kilise, *see* Theotokos hē Panagiotissa
Ka'riye Camii, *see* Christos tēs Chōras
Karpos and Papylos, Hag., 206
Kasim Ağa Mescidi, xvii, 186–89
Kefeli Mescidi, xvii, 36, 190–94, 220
Kemankeş Kara Mustafa Paşa Camii, *see* Odalar Camii
Koca Mustafa Paşa Camii, *see* Atik Mustafa Paşa Camii *and* Andreas en tē Krisei, Hag.
Küçük Ayasofya Camii, *see* Sergios kai Bakchos en tois Hormisdou, Hag.
Kyra Martha, 237

Leo I, emperor, 25
Leo VI, emperor, 322

Manastır Mescidi, 195–99; *see also* Isa Kapısı Mescidi
Mangana Churches, 200–205
Manuel I Comnenus, emperor, 72
Manuel monastery, 190
Maria Ducaena, 41
Maria Palaeologina, 366
Martha, Mary, and Lazarus, Sts. 25
Martha Glabas, 347
Martyrium: Balaban Ağa Mescidi, 25; Euphēmia en tō Hippodromō, 123; Mēnas, Hag., 206; Sophia, Hagia, 265; Iakōbos, Hag., 319
Mary of Constantinople, St., 220
Mausoleum: Christos ho Pantokratōr, 71
Mehmet II, the Conqueror, 71, 231, 315
Mēnas, Hag., 206–8
Mēnodōra, Nymphodōra kai Metrodōra, Hag., 195
Mesihpaşa Camii, *see* Myrelaion
Michaēl, Hag., *see* Christos ho Pantokratōr
Michael VIII, Palaeologus, emperor, 322, 366
Michael Glabas, 347
Mirahor Mescidi, *see* Iōannēs Prodromos en tois Stoudiou, Hag.
Mother-of-God the All-Blessed, *see* Theotokos hē Pammakaristos
Mother-of-God the All-Holy, *see* Theotokos hē Panagiotissa
Mother-of-God of Blachernēs, xvi
Mother-of-God of the Bronzeworkers' District, *see* Theotokos tōn Chalkoprateiōn
Mother-of-God of Lips, *see* Theotokos tou Libos
Mother-of-God the Merciful, *see* Christos ho Pantokratōr
Mother-of-God of the Mongols, *see* Theotokos hē Panagiotissa
Mustafa III, sultan, 315
Myrelaion, 209–19

Nicaea, Koimēsis, 40
Nicholas, St., 190
Nikolaos, Hag., 36

Odalar Camii, 36, 186, 190, 220–24, 189–190

Palace Churches: Hag. Iōannēs en tō Hebdomō, 140; Myrelaion, 209; Hag.

Sergios kai Bakchos, 242; Hagia Sophia, 265
Palermo, Martorana, 237
Pantepoptēs, *see* Christos ho Pantepoptēs
Parekklesion: Christos tēs Chōras, 41; Theotokos hē Pammakaristos, 346–47
Patriarchate, 264, 346
Peter and Paul, Sts., *see* Sergios kai Bakchos, Hag.
Petros kai Markos, Hag., 15
Petros kai Paulos, Hag., *see* Sergios kai Bakchos en tois Hormisdou, Hag.
Philes, 347
Place of Myrrh, *see* Myrelaion
Polyeuktos, Hag., 225–30, 88–89
Polyeuktus, St., *see* Polyeuktos, Hag.
Polykarpos, Hag., 206
Priskos kai Nikolaos, Hag., 376
Procopius, xvi
Pulcheria, empress, 201

Ravenna, S. Vitale, 140
Refectory: Beyazit C, 28
Rhodophylion, 3
Romanos Gate, 195
Romanus Lecapenus, emperor, 209

Sancaktar Hayreddin Mescidi, 231–36
Saraçhane, *see* Polyeuktos, Hag.
Sea Wall, 200
Sekbanbaşı Mescidi, 159, 231, 237–41
Sergios kai Bakchos en tois Hormisdou, Hag., 242–59
Sergius and Bacchus in the Palace of Hormisdas, *see* Sergios kai Bakchos en tois Hormisdou, Hag.
Sinan Paşa Mescidi, 260–61
Skeuophylakion, 262
Sophia, Hagia, xiii, 28, 40, 102, 103, 262–312, 315, 319, 322

Stoudios, senator, 143
Suger of St. Denis, abbot, 263
Şeyh Murat Mescidi, 313–14
Şeyh Süleyman Mescidi, 315–18

Thekla, Hag., 15, 376
Theodora Raoulina, 3, 322
Theodore Metochites, 40–41
Theodoros, Hag., 386
Theodosia en tois Dexiokratous, Hag., 128
Theodosius II, emperor, 123, 262
Theotokos tōn Chalkoprateiōn, 319–21, 383
Theotokos tōn Diakonissēs, 172
Theotokos hē Eleousa, *see* Christos ho Pantokratōr
Theotokos tōn Hodēgōn, 200–201
Theotokos Kecharitomenē, 220
Theotokos ta Kellaraias, 220
Theotokos tou Kouratoros, 25
Theotokos hē Kyriotissa, 172
Theotokos tou Libos, 3, 15, 200, 260, 322–45
Theotokos tōn Hag. Mēnodōra, Nymphodōra kai Metrodōra, 195
Theotokos hē Pammakaristos, 168, 346–65
Theotokos Panagia Mougliotissa, *see* Theotokos hē Panagiotissa
Theotokos hē Panagiotissa, 159, 190, 366–75
Toklu Dede Mescidi, xvii, 376–82
Topkapı Sarayı, 200
Topkapı Sarayı Basilica, 383–85

Valens Aqueduct, 171, 237
Vefa Kilise Camii, 3, 376, 386–401
Venice, San Marco, 225

Zeyrek Camii, *see* Christos ho Pantokratōr

THE
UNIVERSITY OF WINNIPEG
PORTAGE & BALMORAL
WINNIPEG, MAN.   R3B 2E9
CANADA